Faith in the Fire

Faith in the
Fires of Criticism

Christianity in Modern Thought

PAUL AVIS

DARTON·LONGMAN + TODD

First published in 1995 by
Darton, Longman and Todd Ltd
1 Spencer Court
140–142 Wandsworth High Street
London SW18 4JJ

ISBN 0–232–52131–X

A catalogue record for this book is available
from the British Library

ACKNOWLEDGEMENTS

Thanks are due to the following for permission to quote copyright material: Curtis-Brown
for *New and Collected Poems* by Robert Conquest; Faber and Faber Ltd for *Collected Poems
1909 – 1962* by T. S. Eliot and *Collected Poems* by W. H. Auden, edited by Edward Mendelson;
Macmillan General Books for *Later Poems* by R. S. Thomas.

Phototypeset by Intype, London
Printed and bound in Great Britain
by Page Bros, Norwich

Contents

Preface

This book explores the rationality of Christian theology in the modern world. In the past two centuries theology has passed through 'the fires of criticism' – first of the Enlightenment with its challenge to all protected and privileged truth claims, and then of what might be called 'the second enlightenment' of the social sciences as they emerged towards the end of the nineteenth century with their relativist and reductionist thrust. This book does not deal with the Enlightenment as such. Neither does it tackle the question of relativism – the 'relativist proviso' that with the eye of suspicion exposes ideological distortions in all belief and practice. I hope that I may have the opportunity to return to both these vital topics in the future. Instead, this book concentrates on the intense challenge of the great reductionist thinkers to the validity of the Christian faith. The reductionists insisted that theology is grounded in illusion and self-deception, being produced through the psychological mechanism of projection. My aim is to defend the integrity of Christian belief in the face of this 'reductionist veto'.

I call this challenge 'the reductionist veto' because it actually invalidates Christian belief in principle. In the hands of such seminal modern thinkers as Feuerbach, Marx, Nietzsche and Freud, the reductionist approach asserts that the transcendent reality of God, as postulated by theology, can be explained away – reduced to merely human and social factors. For reductionism, theological beliefs form a screen that at the same time both reflects and conceals the real psychological and sociological basis of those beliefs. For this tradition,

the essence of Christianity is merely the essence of humanity.
Now those human and social factors are real enough; nothing
is to be gained by disparaging them. Can theology take them
seriously while continuing to point to a transcendent source
of the sense of God? I argue that it can.

I find my own motivation in writing – and my hopes for
the role of this book – aptly expressed in lines from W. H.
Auden's 'September 1, 1939' (inexplicably excluded by Auden
from the definitive edition of his poems):

> Defenceless under the night
> Our world in stupor lies;
> Yet, dotted everywhere,
> Ironic points of light
> Flash out wherever the Just
> Exchange their messages.

In this book, the just, with their ironic points of light, are
the witnesses to truths that the Christian Church did not
want to hear – Feuerbach, Marx, Nietzsche, Freud, Jung,
Horkheimer, Adorno and others. Christianity can draw
enlightenment from their critiques without subscribing to all
their conclusions.

I also make Auden's aspiration to witness to light and truth
my own.

> May I, composed like them
> Of Eros and of dust,
> Beleaguered by the same
> Negation and despair,
> Show an affirming flame.
>   (Skelton, p. 283)

My hope is that, in the pages that follow, the fires of criticism,
bravely endured, may be transmuted into Auden's affirming
flame!

This short book has occupied me for a number of years. I
have worked on it intermittently while other projects have
come along and been completed. I have persevered with it in
this way because I am convinced that few things are more
important for Christian theology and Christian belief today
than to listen with an open mind to the most damning things
that modern thinkers have had to say about Christianity and

to ask ourselves to what extent they have been justified and whether they have said the last word. Clearly, I believe that the views of the great reductionist thinkers are not the final judgement on Christianity, though I hold that the traditional faith will be radically changed in certain respects if we take to heart what they say where it has the ring of truth.

I would like to acknowledge once again the invaluable secretarial help of Gillian Piper without whom the difficulties of producing the text through a succession of drafts would have become oppressive indeed.

PAUL AVIS
Stoke Canon Vicarage, Exeter

1

Theology as Illusion:
the Reductionist Veto

The only hope, or else despair
Lies in the choice of pyre or pyre –
To be redeemed from fire by fire.
(T. S. ELIOT, p. 221; 'Little Gidding')

Theology was once the crown of human thought, the Queen of the Sciences. It gave true, objective knowledge of divine mysteries and of the reality of our human condition. For St Thomas Aquinas in the thirteenth century, theology drew on sources of truth grounded in the mind and being of God and disclosed in divine revelation (*S. T.* Ia, I, 2, *Resp.*). According to John Calvin at the Reformation, true wisdom consists of the knowledge of God and of ourselves: both are taught by Christian theology through exegesis of inspired Scripture (*Institutes*, I, 1, *1*). Today traditionalist Christians still believe that theology operates by a sort of direct reading off of the data of divine revelation which exists 'out there', as an objective, unadulterated body of meaning with its own rationality, coherence and integrity.

Fundamentalist Christians locate this revelation in the written text of the Bible, taking all parts as equally authoritative and divinely inspired in every detail. More sophisticated Protestants, following Karl Barth, postulate a real but somehow elusive revelation embodied in the person and work of Jesus Christ, but identical with neither the text of Scripture nor the teaching of the Church. Conservative Roman Catholic theology, kept in order by the Vatican, still upholds a propositional view of revelation – a revelation given in Scripture and tradition but entrusted to the care and interpretation of the living magisterium of the Catholic Church, presided over by the pope.

Is this traditional view of theology tenable any more? How

has it fared in the modern world? Has it survived the critical
scrutiny of the Enlightenment and the more recent social
sciences? If not, at what points has it been found wanting?
Can it undergo a sort of refit – like those modern leviathans
the Polaris submarines – when it begins to creak at the seams,
to rehabilitate it along traditional lines, or is more drastic
attention called for? Can Christian theology – having passed
through the fires of criticism for more than two centuries –
be reconstructed so that it can still speak to us of the things
of God and hold out guidance and inspiration for the spiritual
life? This is the challenge that this book attempts to face with
a positive intent. But the road to constructive restatement
must first pass through the desert of critical negation as
we turn our attention to the most unsparing critics of the
theological enterprise.

For a succession of some of the most influential modern
thinkers, Christian theology is fundamentally misguided. It
is in fact completely invalid. For them, Christianity is essentially illusory – merely a projection on a cosmic scale of
processes going on within the human psyche and human
society. For Feuerbach, Marx, Nietzsche and Freud, in particular, theology reflects, not a transcendent sacred reality,
however dimly apprehended, but merely human fears and
longings. These seminal thinkers of our modern world raise
the crucial question: is the essence of Christianity merely the
essence of humanity itself? The challenge, to which we are
addressing ourselves in this book, has perhaps never been
more astringently formulated than by Ludwig Feuerbach
(1804–72) who claimed that 'the objective essence of religion,
particularly the Christian religion, is nothing but the essence
of human, and particularly Christian feelings.' The 'secret of
theology', Feuerbach triumphantly concluded, 'is therefore
anthropology.'

For Friedrich Nietzsche (1844–1900), similarly, Christianity was a retreat from reality – 'a form of mortal hostility
to reality as yet unsurpassed' (A-X, p. 139) – into a 'purely
fictitious world' (p. 125). As Nietzsche wrote in *The Antichrist*, his most explicit attack on the Christian religion:

In Christianity neither morality nor religion come into
contact with reality at any point. Nothing but imaginary

causes ('God', 'soul' . . . 'spirit' . . .): nothing but imaginary *effects* ('sin', 'redemption', 'grace', 'punishment',
'forgiveness of sins'). A traffic between imaginary *beings*
('God', 'spirits', 'souls'); an imaginary *natural* science
(anthropocentric; complete lack of the concept of
natural causes); an imaginary *psychology* (. . . interpretations of pleasant or unpleasant general feelings . . . with
the aid of the sign-language of religio-moral idiosyn-
cracy – 'repentance', 'sting of conscience', 'temptation
by the Devil', 'the proximity of God'); an imaginary
teleology ('the kingdom of God', 'the Last Judgement',
'eternal life'). (p. 125)

For the reductionists, Christianity is a great delusional
system of ideas generated by means of 'projection'. They
indict Christianity for preferring false hope and deny the
comfort it offers. They eliminate the transcendent and con-
front the world in its naked contingency. As a contemporary
poet, Robert Conquest, puts it:

> The world is as it is. There is no helpful answer,
> No saving parable or spell that can be told
> In blinding rhetorics of star or rainbow.

Theirs is an austere but not ignoble creed:

> Our only hope must be the truly human.
>   (Conquest, pp. 38f)

In the face of meaninglessness, they make an act of personal
commitment; in place of grace, they offer finite, human love.
For example, Freud described psychoanalysis as 'a cure
through love'. Adorno spoke of the ideal of 'non-possessive
devotion'. So Conquest writes:

> And against the universe I can only put love;
> Against the constellations of despair can only
> Give you my hand and sooner or later die
> – Or am I wrong?

This book aims to answer that question, 'Am I wrong?' gently
but firmly, in the affirmative.

The Projection of the Human World

The psychological mechanism that renders this radical critique nothing less then a 'reductionist veto' is that of 'projection'. What is meant by 'projection'? It is defined by Rycroft as 'the process by which specific impulses, wishes, aspects of the self, or internal objects are imagined to be located in some object external to oneself' (pp. 125f; cf., Jung, *CW*, 6, p. 457). We speak properly of projection only when the transfer of subjective psychic contents on to an outer reality is unconscious, that is to say, unperceived and unintentional (von Franz, p. 3).

Projection plays a part in the normal development of the individual and in the construction of social reality. Projection is not in itself pathological, though the same mechanism underlies many manifestations of psychopathology. Projection takes place in all human going forth into the world, in perception, action and communication. Peter Berger describes the constitution of perceived reality in the three stages of externalisation, objectivation and internalisation:

> Externalisation is the ongoing outpouring of human being into the world, both in the physical and the mental activity of men. Objectivation is the attainment by the products of this activity (again both physical and mental) of a reality that confronts its original producers as a facticity external to and other than themselves. Internalisation is the reappropriation by men of this same reality, transforming it once again from structures of the objective world into structures of the subjective consciousness. (1973, p. 14)

However, where human beings are fundamentally alienated from themselves, projection is distorted. Unacceptable, 'bad', cut off, irrational parts of the psyche are projected on to the screen of external reality – on to others, the world and God. These projections are then available to be ingested, introjected, back into the psyche to produce guilt, aggression, or depression. Negative projections are therefore a function of inner alienation, a fruit of the human condition in need of redemption.

Projection forms the link between individual and social

psychology, between the constraints that impinge on the process of individuation and the constraints that affect the pattern of social change. Here I want to consider the individual aspects of projection, that is, in relation to personality; I cannot begin to explore the collective, social dimension of projection, that is, in relation to ideology – though this is to abstract two related aspects of a single mechanism that operates at both the individual and the social levels. There is not only an analogy but a causal connection between individual projection and socio-political ideology. As Jung puts it: 'Just as we tend to assume that the world is as we see it, we naively suppose that people are as we imagine them to be.' While with regard to the external world there are scientific procedures of verification or falsification that will reveal the discrepancy between perception and reality, with regard to the world of personal relationships we are often content to take our projections at face value. 'Although the possibility of gross deception is infinitely greater here than in our perception of the physical world, we still go on naively projecting our own psychology into our fellow human beings. In this way everyone creates for himself a series of more or less imaginary relationships based essentially on projection' (Jung, 1985, p. 50).

According to Jung, projection belongs to the stage of archaic identification of subject and object, in which reality is perceived through a veil of illusion. When this identity becomes disturbing and no longer measures up to the demands of the situation, projections begin to be withdrawn, the first step in the long process of the disenchantment of the world (Jung CW, 6, p. 457). But as projections are withdrawn from outer reality into the psyche, from whence they originated, they activate the archetypal images, so enriching subjective experience and providing the conditions for the lifelong process of individuation (CW, 5, p. 89; cf., 1983b, p. 133). Primitive humans, babies and neurotics are largely at the mercy of their projections. According to Jung, 'Primitive man has a minimum of self-awareness combined with a maximum of attachment to the object; hence the object can exercise a direct magical compulsion upon him. All primitive magic and religion are based on these magical attachments,

which simply consist in the projection of unconscious contents into the object' (1985, p. 56).

Enlightenment comes to the primitive in the process of
taming the environment; to the infant as the work of discrimi-
nating self and other, inner needs and outward reality,
advances; to the neurotic through analysis in which, through
the phenomenon of transference, the analyst becomes the
bearer of both positive and negative projections derived from
early experiences, which then become distinguished and
detached from the unconscious and can be recognised for
what they are.

In Freud's view – which was formed not only from his
reading of anthropological literature but also from a postulated parallel between 'the phases in the development of men's
view of the universe and the stages of an individual's libidinal
development' (*PFL*, 13, p. 148) – primitive religion or animism was an aspect of this projection of mind on to reality,
and late Western religions – Christian and Judaic – were a
more sophisticated and conceptually elaborated form of the
same psychological mechanism, a 'return of the repressed' in
the history of the race (pp. 372ff). For Freud, psychoanalysis,
which reveals the subjective projections that can lead to neurosis, can also, through extrapolation, and in alliance with
anthropology, uncover the projection mechanisms underlying
religion today and liberate us from them – and it. As Freud
puts it: 'Primitive man transposed the structural conditions
of his own mind into the external world, and we may attempt
to reverse the process and put back into the human mind
what animism teaches as to the nature of things' (p. 149).

Babies and neurotics have in common what Freud calls
'the omnipotence of thoughts' – subjective feelings tend to
swamp objective impressions. Freud regards this as a
regression (in the case of neurotics) to a primitive mode of
thinking. He finds it most prominently in obsessional neurosis, though in all types of neurosis that reveal this phenomenon 'what determines the formation of symptoms is the
reality not of experience but of thought'. Such neurotics,
Freud points out, 'live in a world apart where ... only "neurotic currency" is legal tender; that is to say, they are only
affected by what is thought with intensity and pictured with
emotion, whereas agreement with external reality is a matter

of no importance' (*PFL*, 13, p. 144). As Freud further insists: 'What lie behind the sense of guilt of neurotics are always *psychical* realities and never *factual* ones. What characterises neurotics is that they prefer psychical to factual reality and react just as seriously to thoughts as normal people do to realities' (p. 222). To constantly preserve the mental adjustment that this fact requires is the first secret of analysis:

> One must never allow oneself to be misled into applying the standards of reality to repressed psychical structures, and, on that account, perhaps, into undervaluing the importance of phantasies in the formation of symptoms on the ground that they are not actualities, or into tracing a neurotic sense of guilt back to some other source because there is no evidence that any actual crime has been committed. One is bound to employ the currency that is in use in the country one is exploring – in our case a neurotic currency. (*PFL*, p. 43)

Horkheimer and Adorno employ the Freudian concept of morbid projection, in conjunction with the Marxist critique of ideology, as a critical tool against Fascism and authoritarianism. Morbid projection consists of the transference of socially taboo impulses from the subject to the object. Under pressure from the super-ego (the disapproving conscience), the ego projects the aggressive or lascivious impulses that emerge from the instinctual reservoir of the id on to others, reading them as evil intentions directed against itself. In responding violently to these supposed evil intentions, the individual is rejecting an unacceptable part of himself. 'The sick individual regresses to the archaic non-differentiation of love and domination. He is concerned with physical proximity, seizure-relationship at all costs. Since he cannot allow himself the pleasure of following his own instincts, he attacks other individuals in envy or persecution just as the repressed bestialist hunts or torments an animal' (Horkheimer & Adorno 1973, p. 192).

True projection is the active, outgoing aspect in all perception – what Horkheimer and Adorno, following Auerbach, calls mimesis. Mimesis is controlled projection, and preserves the epistemic distance between the subject and the object.

Morbid projection is in thrall to uncontrolled instinctual forces:

> Mimesis imitates the environment, but false projection makes the environment like itself. For mimesis the outside world is a model which the inner world must try to conform to: the alien must become familiar; but false projection confuses the inner and outer world and defines the most intimate experiences as hostile. Impulses which the subject will not admit as his own . . . are attributed to the object – the prospective victim. (Horkheimer & Adorno 1973, p. 187)

Anti-semitism is the archetypal form of morbid projection, and in Fascism a psychological mechanism is given political legitimation and institutional embodiment: 'the object of the illness is deemed true to reality, and the mad system becomes the reasonable norm . . . and deviation from it a neurosis' (Horkheimer & Adorno 1973, p. 187). It is as though Freud's discovery of primitive sexual impulses – aggressive, destructive, devouring – and Marx's discovery of the introjection of reified social processes into the consciousness as ideology, were prophetic of the evil forces that Nazism unleashed upon the world. This is presumably what Horkheimer and Adorno intend in the cryptic statement: 'The same sexual impulses which the human species suppressed have survived and prevailed – in individuals and in nations – by way of the mental conversion of the ambient world into a diabolical system' (ibid.).

If I have laboured the pathological manifestations of projection, it is because they present us with the clearest evidence of a mechanism that is operative, to a lesser extent in us all. Our apprehension of reality as basically either hostile or benevolent is not only a rational judgement formed in response to the way life has treated us, but very largely a projection of infantile experiences. Children whose trust has been broken, whose love has been unrequited and whose security has been shattered will often grow up to see the world as threatening. They will have a chip on their shoulder, and understandably so. But the irrational fears of the most balanced of people originate in such infantile experiences or disciplines. As Erikson writes:

The human being in early childhood learns to consider one or the other aspect of bodily function as evil, shameful or unsafe. There is no culture which does not use a combination of these devils to develop, by way of counterpoint, its own style of faith, pride, certainty and initiative. There thus remains in man's sense of achievement the suspicion of its infantile roots; and since his earliest sense of reality was learned by the painful testing of inner and outer goodnesses and badnesses, man remains ready to expect from some enemy, force or event in the outer world that which, in fact, endangers him from within: from his own angry drives, from his own sense of smallness, and from his own split inner world.

Thus, concludes Erikson, 'he is always irrationally ready to fear invasion by vast and vague forces which are other than himself' (1977, p. 365).

Our knowledge of the physical and human worlds is built up as projections are recognised for what they are and withdrawn from their object. Projection cannot be eliminated but, as Jung suggests, the sciences have 'subtilised' their projections 'to an almost unrecognisable degree', while ordinary life and human relationships still swarm with them (CW, 11, p. 83). As the manifestation of unconscious processes, projections must be recognised and taken account of if they are not to lead to an increasing alienation from reality culminating in neurosis.

The effect of projection is to isolate the subject from his environment, since instead of a real relation to it there is now only an illusory one. Projections change the world into the replica of one's unknown face. In the last analysis, therefore, they lead to an autoerotic or autistic condition in which one dreams a world whose reality remains forever unattainable. (Jung CW, 9, ii, p. 9)

The dark forces created by projection take various alien embodiments in different cultures: devils, witches, negroes, communists, liberal theologians, women priests . . .

Thus men in slavery of sorrow imagine ghastly creeds.
(Bridges, p. 59)

The fears are dispelled by enlightenment, by knowledge: the knowledge that there are no devils or witches, as traditionally imagined, though there are destructive unconscious forces; the knowledge that black races and white races share a common human nature; the knowledge that liberals in theology are often men and women of prayer and faith; the knowledge of the composite character of our own sexuality and of the androgynous psychological qualities of the most integrated and fulfilled individuals, which evacuates the threat posed by the apparent 'otherness' of women in a patriarchal culture. Above all it is self-knowledge, enlightenment, that enables the mature individual to discriminate between objective reality and the 'objectification' of reality through the mechanism of projection.

In his poem 'The Flower', R. S. Thomas describes a process akin to this withdrawal of projections from the external world and their absorption into the psyche:

> I asked riches.
> You gave me the earth, the sea,
> the immensity
> of the broad sky. I looked at them
> and learned I must withdraw
> to possess them. I gave my eyes
> and my ears, and dwelt
> in a soundless darkness
> in the shadow
> of your regard.

The result of this withdrawal is an enrichment of the inner life and an enhancement of its sense of God:

> The soul
> grew in me, filling me
> with its fragrance.
> Men came
> to me from the four
> winds to hear me speak
> of the unseen flower by which
> I sat, whose roots were not
> in the soil, nor its petals the colour
> of the wide sea; that was

its own species with its own
sky over it, shot
with the rainbow of your coming and going.

(R. S. Thomas, p. 63)

Precursors of Projection

The concept of projection is a sophisticated version of the
ancient wisdom of humanity that perceived our insatiable
capacity for making all things, even gods, in our own image.
The second commandment, the prohibition of idolatry,
reflects this inveterate tendency of human nature. In modern
thought theories of projection (though it is anachronistic to
call them this before the mid-nineteenth century) can be
divided into pre-Kantian and post-Kantian. I would like to
set the scene by illustrating pre-Kantian notions of projection
from the writings of Bacon, Vico and Hume, before going
on to develop in greater depth modern ideas of projection
in the thought of Feuerbach, Marx, Nietzsche, Freud, the
Frankfurt school, the sociology of knowledge and, finally,
Jung.

Francis Bacon (1561–1626)

Bacon's general theory of perception is the antithesis of
Kant's, but his notion of the idols of the mind is certainly an
early contribution to the concept of projection. Bacon held
out the possibility of totally objective thinking. He believed
in the unmediated correspondence of mind and nature. 'All
depends,' he urges, 'on keeping the eye steadily fixed upon
the facts of nature and so receiving their images simply as
they are.' His ideal is 'an apocalypse or true vision of the
footsteps of the Creator imprinted on his creatures' (1905,
pp. 253f). 'What I purpose', Bacon declares in words that
seem to pre-empt Kant, 'is to unite you with *things themselves* in a chaste, holy and legal wedlock' (1964, p. 72, original emphasis). Bacon's claims have all the appearance of a
calculated prophetic provocation to later theories of knowledge. 'I am building in the human understanding a true model
of the world, such as it is in fact, not such as man's own
reason would have it to be' (1905, p. 298; Avis 1986b, pp. 63f).

Bacon does not of course believe that we already enjoy this pure and undistorted gaze but he holds it out as attainable through his revolutionary method. As things stand, the deductive approach and syllogistic logic of the scholastics have made the mind of man 'like an enchanted glass, full of superstition and imposture' (1915, p. 132). As a result, we are substituting 'a dream of our own imagination for a pattern of the world' (1905, pp. 253f). If, however, the mind has the innate capacity for pure and undistorted perception, this present sorry state of knowledge must be due, not to some logical or epistemological necessity, but to 'accidental' psychological deficiency. Perception of reality is warped, not by any inherent categories of the mind that impose a pattern on things, but by aberrations of the will as 'feeling penetrates and infects thinking', by particular interests and prejudices – or, as we would say, by projection. These interests or prejudices are Bacon's idols: those of the tribe, representing the interests of the species; those of the cave, the interests of the individual; those of the market-place, the interests of social life, and communicative structures; and finally, those of the theatre, the interests, prejudices and fallacies of the philosophers.

Bacon's terminology contains a tacit allusion to the second commandment, and it is indeed with regard to religion that the idols are most baneful in Bacon's view. Superstition and blind zeal are the enemies not only of natural philosophy but of true religion. As Bacon pronounces in his essay 'Of Superstition' (1890, p. 2), 'It were better to have no opinion of God at all than such an opinion as is unworthy of him.' Superstition is thus worse than atheism because it projects an unworthy image of deity. Superstition is a danger to the individual and to society. It erects 'an absolute monarchy in the minds of men', a sovereign delusion, an all-embracing ideology which is destructive of social orders: 'The master of superstition is the people; and in all superstition wise men follow fools; and arguments are fitted to practice, in a reversed order.'

Giambattista Vico (1688–1744)

Vico, who looked, though not uncritically, to Bacon as one of his supreme mentors, has his own theory of projection, summed up in the phrases 'the conceit of nations' and 'the conceit of scholars'. These are the illusions, respectively, that all nations have of their superiority and of the inferiority of other nations, and the gratifying self-assurance of academics that they are in possession of the wisdom of the ages, that Plato, Aristotle or whoever, endorses their opinion. For Vico, both errors rest on the human failings of anthropomorphism and anachronism. Humanity characteristically attempts to bring the unknown into line with the known. We project the present on to the past, mind on to nature. 'Because of the indefinite nature of the human mind, wherever it is lost in ignorance man makes himself the measure of all things' (Vico, para. 120). As I have shown elsewhere, this perception has enormous heuristic and methodological importance for Vico, effectively undermining a whole gamut of scholarly assumptions in the field of historical and cultural science (Avis 1986b, p. 146). We shall return to Vico at the end of this book.

David Hume (1711–1776)

Though discrimination between reality and illusion is as old as the human mind, it was the special work of the Enlightenment before Kant – and long before Marx and Freud – to reveal the difference between things as they seem and things as they are, and to expose privilege and oppression under the disguise of 'nature' and 'providence'. The sleight of hand that effects this transference is the mechanism of projection. Hume too was aware of it: 'There is a universal tendency among mankind to conceive of all beings like themselves, and to transfer to every object those qualities with which they are familiarly acquainted, and of which they are intimately conscious,' he asserts in *The Natural History of Religion* adding, 'We find human faces in the moon, armies in the clouds; and by a natural propensity, if not corrected by experience and reflection, ascribe malice or goodwill to everything that hurts or pleases us' (p. 137). But it took the 'Copernican revolution' of Immanuel Kant (d. 1804) to provide a conceptualisation in the realm of epistemology for the familiar phenomenon of projection. Kant's principle that mind has the making of reality, construing it according to certain inherent mental structures or 'categories' is the presupposition of the modern theory of projection. In the nineteenth and twentieth centuries, the theory of projection has been developed in several directions: by Hegel into a metaphysical principle of objectification or externalisation, and building on this, by Feuerbach, Marx, Nietzsche and Freud into a radical demolition of religion that went far beyond Hegel. In Jung we find a more nuanced, even ambivalent interpretation of religion in which the therapeutic value of the withdrawal of projections and their absorption into the psyche is stressed.

2
Christianity's Baptism of Fire:
Ludwig Feuerbach

A seminal influence on the thinking of those arch-reduction-ists of the Christian religion – Friedrich Nietzsche and Sigmund Freud – was Feuerbach; whose significance for the deconstruction of traditional metaphysics and theology was earlier pointed up by Karl Marx. Though himself a critic of Feuerbach, and acutely conscious of his limitations, Marx heralded Feuerbach's place of primacy in the unapostolic succession of thinkers who had negated the transcendental truth claims of Christian theology and its allied metaphysic.

In words that have become well known, Marx rubs the noses of theologians in the unpalatable challenge presented by Feuerbach to religion:

> And to you, speculative philosophers and theologians, I give you this advice: free yourselves from the concepts and prejudices of previous speculative philosophy if you also wish to attain to things as they are, that is, to the truth. And there is no other way for you to truth and freedom than through the stream of fire [the *Feuerbach*]. Feuerbach is the purgatory of the present time. (Marx 1972, p. 25)

The unintended irony in Marx's advice is that neither Marx nor Feuerbach did succeed in freeing themselves from 'previous speculative philosophy' (i.e. Hegelianism). In fact they were both worthy exponents of the master's (Hegel's) dialectical method – the transformations of thought and being according to the pattern of unity, contradiction, reconciliation;

thesis, antithesis, synthesis. It was merely the content that changed (see Kee, part 1).

Biographical Background (1804–1872)

Ludwig Feuerbach was born in 1804 in Landshut, Bavaria, the son of an eminent jurist, and grew up in a liberal and enlightened family atmosphere. He studied theology at Heidelberg, where he found the rationalistic tone of much of the theological fare unsatisfying. Moving to Berlin, he sat at the feet of the greatest creative theological minds of the first half of the nineteenth century – Hegel and Schleiermacher. Feuerbach went on to gain his doctorate at Erlangen where the cost of living was lower than in Berlin, but his hopes of a university career were dashed by the unfavourable reaction to his first post-doctoral publication, the subversive *Thoughts on Death and Immortality* (1830). The failure of his academic aspirations seems merely to have fuelled his intense philosophical ambition, and marriage to a wealthy industrialist enabled him to work in splendid isolation – almost literally in an ivory tower – on his wife's estate. Three volumes on the history of philosophy appeared in the 1830s – the first covering the period from Francis Bacon to Spinoza, the second on Leibniz and the third on Pierre Bayle. Feuerbach followed this with a critique of Hegelian philosophy as a prelude to his devastating attack on Christianity, *The Essence of Christianity* (1841). Feuerbach continued to pour forth writings, including *The Essence of Religion* (1845) and works on mythologies and world religions until his death in comparative poverty in 1872.

Critique of Philosophy

The river of fire that purges our metaphysical illusions, according to Marx, is Feuerbach's celebrated method of inversion or transposition. Feuerbach stands the fundamental assumptions of the Western philosophical tradition up to Hegel on their head; he turns them inside out. He inverts transcendence and immanence, heaven and earth, God and humanity. Hegel had employed the concept of projection or objectification (*Vergegenstandlichung*) to describe how God, the Absolute, perpetually pours itself out into the finite realm in creation. Feuerbach simply reverses this and claims that 'the Absolute' is merely a projection, an objectification, of humanity. He applies this formula first to philosophy and then to theology.

Feuerbach is above all a critic of philosophy – the first and greatest of modern critics of philosophy outside the positivist tradition, according to Wartofsky's judgement in his magisterial exposition of Feuerbach's thought (Wartofsky, p. 2). While Hegel sees the development of philosophy as the Absolute coming to a knowledge of itself, almost as a self-revelation of the Absolute through the process of dialectic, Feuerbach interprets the philosophical tradition as solely a human activity, a highly evolved mode of human self-understanding, yet one that is hidden from its subjects. Through mechanisms of self-deception the essentially human content of philosophy is masked by the metaphysical, transcendental-ist façade. Philosophy is an esoteric form of the knowledge of human nature expressed in deceptive abstractions. The 'forms of life', of social or species nature, of which Hegel had spoken, were not expressions or embodiments of metaphysical reality – they were the ultimate, merely human reality of which metaphysics was the projection. Under this analysis, philosophy as traditionally understood dissolves and becomes instead the purely scientific, naturalistic study of human nature and the reflective elaboration of the conditions of human life (Wartofsky, p. 3).

Philosophy is thus unmasked as the abstract, metaphysical representation of fundamental human needs. This is the highest point of the conceptual elaboration of human aspirations. It presupposes the reflective constructions of theology which present human needs in an abstruse and esoteric form. In its turn theology presupposes actual religion in which these same mundane human needs are first subjected to sensuous, imaginative and symbolic representation. Theology builds on religion, and philosophy builds on theology. As Feuerbach says: 'The secret of philosophy is theology' and 'the secret of theology is anthropology' (Wartofsky, p. 3).

Feuerbach reverses Hegel's notion of the Absolute coming to a knowledge of itself through its self-objectification in finite reality. For Feuerbach, it is humans who come to a knowledge of themselves through projection or objectification. This process of gradual self-knowledge is only possible through our self-objectification as something other than and greater than human – God, Nature or Being. Speculative philosophy is therefore the continuation of theology by other means, the study of God transformed into the study of Being. If theology is abstract and esoteric religion, philosophy is abstract and esoteric theology – and is therefore doubly abstract and esoteric. The distinctive method and approach of philosophy is to strip away the still personal, still sensuously conceived aspects of the divine image in humanity, as theology understands it, until only the most severely logical and metaphysical attributes remain – which are then in turn reconceived as attributes of a hypostatised impersonal Being. It is true to say, therefore, that for Feuerbach philosophy merely perpetuates the mystification and conceptual inversion that is typical of theology. 'God' and 'Being' are equally images of the infinity, universality and unity of the collective reality (or 'species-being') of humanity. Feuerbach was not guilty of treating religion frivolously: he took it seriously as a necessary stage – though one that was destined to be superseded – in the emergence of human self-understanding (Wartofsky, pp. 4–6).

Critique of Theology

Feuerbach's critical reduction of Christianity in *The Essence of Christianity* presupposes this prior demolition of the objective claims of philosophy, of metaphysics. While, for Feuerbach, religion is indeed the means whereby the human species progressively comes to a knowledge of its own essential nature, in so doing it is mistaking self-consciousness for the consciousness of an objective reality. Through conscious reflection, these projections of its own emerging attributes are hypostatised into the theological attributes of God. Thus for Feuerbach, 'theology is nothing but esoteric anthropology.' (Clearly Feuerbach is not dealing with the immediate content of religious consciousness, which is a matter of acting, believing and feeling, but with the reflective elaboration of this in theology; the Christianity in *The Essence of Christianity* is Christian theology.) The polarity of humanity and divinity represents the tension between humanity's present alienated existence and its true essence (Wartofsky, p. 199). Through a twofold process of objectification and reappropriation, of projection and introjection, humanity builds up the picture of its essential identity:

> Man – this is the mystery of religion – projects his being into objectivity, and then again makes himself an object to this projected image of himself thus converted into a subject; he thinks of himself as an object to himself, but as the object of an object, of another being than himself. (Feuerbach 1957, p. 30)

God is then 'the highest subjectivity of man abstracted from himself' and then reintegrated. Feuerbach likens this process to the contraction and expansion of the heart. 'In the religious systole man propels his own nature from himself, he throws himself outward; in the religious diastole he receives the rejected nature into his heart again' (Feuerbach 1957, p. 31). Humanity has constructed God in its own image – though one that is concealed from humanity. As Hans Küng has summed it up: 'the truth of religion consists in the equation of divine and human predicates; its untruth, in the attempt to distinguish these' (Küng 1980, p. 202). The alienation of humanity's true nature has resulted in a drastic impoverishment of human existence. In a perverse parody of the theological concept of *kenosis* (self-emptying), humanity has dispossessed itself of its true spiritual wealth and poured its treasures at the feet of the God figment.

Feuerbach reinterprets the whole of Christian theology by means of his (to him) blindingly obvious formula. The mind of God is the projection of the human understanding; the commandments of God are the projection of the human moral nature; the love of God is the projection of human compassion. The incarnation, for example, is the manifestation of humanity's projection of its nature on to God. The Holy Trinity merely mirrors human sociality. The Word of God (Logos) represents the deification of the human capacity for reasoned speech. The resurrection reflects the human longing for personal immortality – and so on.

In his *Lectures on the Essence of Religion*, Feuerbach reviewed his writings, especially those on the essence of

Christianity and the essence of religion, and summed up his life's work – the demolition of Christianity and the substitution of a new faith in the future of humanity based on harmony with nature. Nature stands for wholeness of existence, and the physical and sensuous aspect of nature is reflected in religion, which is sensuous and aesthetic and therefore superior to philosophy, which is bloodless and abstract (Feuerbach 1967, pp. 4, 12f). 'The first gospels, the first and most reliable documents of human religion, unfalsified by clerical fraud, are man's senses' (p. 87).

It is religion, not philosophy, that is the foundation of human life, and of ethics and politics. Unlike Marx, Feuerbach does not anticipate a time when religion as such will completely fade away. Rather, he looks forward to an enlightened religion of humanity. It has been his purpose, he declares, 'to demonstrate that the powers which man worships and fears in his religious life, which he seeks to propitiate even with bloody human sacrifices, are merely creatures of his own unfree, fearful mind, and of his ignorant, unformed intelligence'. The purpose of his books and lectures, he confesses, 'is to transform theologians into anthropologists, lovers of God into lovers of man, candidates for the next world into students of this world' (Feuerbach 1967, pp. 22f). 'True atheism' is not merely a denial; it is an affirmation: 'it negates the being abstracted from man . . . but only in order to replace him by man's true being' (p. 282).

Feuerbach frankly acknowledged his own religious disposition: 'Though I myself am an atheist, I openly profess religion in the sense [of] . . . nature religion. I hate the idealism that wrenches man out of nature; I am not ashamed of my dependency on nature' (Feuerbach 1967, p. 35). 'Even today,' he disarmingly admits, 'I find *within myself* the motives of natural religion, motives which, if they were not countered by culture, science and philosophy, would still make me a nature worshipper today' (p. 90). Again: 'I do not deny religion, I do not deny the subjective, human foundations of religion, namely, feeling and imagination and man's impulse to objectify and personify his inner life . . . I merely deny the object of religion' (p. 181).

Looking back on *The Essence of Christianity*, Feuerbach reaffirmed its thesis that God is the deified essence of man and theology is anthropology, but he acknowledged a significant gap in his analysis. That book had ignored nature – simply because Christianity itself does. Christianity is a form of idealism. It is interested in God only as a moral being. But the essence of humanity presupposes our natural existence; the projection of this essence into deity should, therefore, reflect this fact (Feuerbach 1967, pp. 17, 19). In *The Essence of Religion*, Feuerbach had argued that when God is regarded as the cause of nature, God expresses the deified, personified essence of nature. He reverses the 'universal doctrine in an upside-down world that nature sprang from God'; on the contrary, the concept of God was an abstraction from nature. Feuerbach must therefore amend his definition of theology: it is not only anthropology but also physiology (pp. 21, 103).

In this later work, *The Essence of Religion*, Feuerbach had argued (following Schleiermacher) that the foundation of religion is a feeling of dependence. The first object of this feeling of dependence is nature; therefore nature itself is the primary object of religion. Nature includes the animal kingdom, and where animals are worshipped it is because humanity tends to deify those beings or things on which it believes its life depends. The notion of God's goodness is 'merely abstracted from those beings and phenomena in nature which are useful, good and helpful to man'. We are still worshipping ourselves in animals. The value that humanity sets on itself – human egotism – is at the root of religion. For unless we first love and worship ourselves, how can we love and worship what benefits us? 'How shall I believe in an *outward* God unless I have an inner, subjective God?' What is this inner deity? It is the aggregate of all human drives, needs and predispositions; it is human existence, human life (Feuerbach 1967, pp. 49, 51f, 111). However, the ultimate aim of religion is to free humanity from that dependence that forms the ground of religion (p. 207). This freedom will be achieved in immortality. The hope of immortality is the ultimate motive for belief in God and we love the God who will give us eternal life (p. 267).

Elaborating his basic thesis that religion is the projection of human feelings, Feuerbach suggests that whereas polytheists need a whole pantheon to represent the various religious feelings, Christians are able to distribute those feel-

ings among the attributes of the one God. The sense of
dependence includes love, joy and fear, but Feuerbach (like
Nietzsche) makes the last dominant: 'Just as evil spirits are
virtually the sole objects of the worship of primitive peoples,
so the angry God is the chief object of worship among Christian peoples'(Feuerbach 1967, p. 29). Feuerbach pours scorn
on those rational theologians who play down the supernatural, interventionist and miraculous aspects of Christianity to
comply with the demands of reason and the moral sense.
Their God is unworthy of the name (p. 149). Here we gain
a strong impression that Feuerbach's attack on Christianity
depends on setting up an Aunt Sally that can then be demol-
ished. Feuerbach will not allow us to question his caricature.
By insisting that his portrait of Christianity is the only valid
one, he excludes all the great liberal theologians since Schleiermacher from his picture of Christian theology.

It is the human imagination that creates anthropomorphic
divine beings out of these elemental feelings. 'It is the imagination that creates man's gods.' God 'is merely the hypostati-
zed and objectified essence of the human imagination'
(Feuerbach 1967, pp. 136, 177). Our imagination reflects our
nature: a gloomy, fearful man imagines terrifying gods; a
serene, happy man imagines friendly gods. Therefore the gods
of humanity are as diverse as human nature itself (p. 188).
The more humanity is dominated by the imagination, the
more sensuous are its gods; the more humanity learns to think
in abstract concepts, the more impersonal and sophisticated
becomes its concept of God (p. 192). 'As man is, so is his
god' (p. 232).

Assessment of Feuerbach in Modern Theology

Feuerbach once proclaimed that the task of the modern age
was 'the humanization of God'(Küng 1980, p. 199). Karl
Barth saw this conversion as the rationale of the decadent
progress of modern theology. Feuerbach merely pushed to
its logical conclusion what was latent in Hegel and Schleiermacher: he 'sought to take Schleiermacher and Hegel seriously,
completely seriously, at the point where they concurred in
asserting the non-objective quality of God . . . to turn
theology, which itself seemed half inclined towards the same

goal, completely and finally into anthropology' (Barth 1972, p. 534). Barth points out that this was Feuerbach's own interpretation of the logic of Protestant theology – it had 'long since become anthropology', from the moment in particular when Luther and Melanchthon 'ceased to be interested in what God is in himself and became emphatically interested in what God is for man' (p. 536).

Barth traced the Protestant identification of deity and humanity to the Lutheran interpretation of the doctrine of the *communicatio idiomatum* in Christology – the interchange of divine and human properties in the person of the incarnate Jesus Christ. This amounted to an 'apotheosis of human nature'. Barth asked: 'Was Hegel so wrong after all when he thought that he could profess to be a good Lutheran? Was it mere impudence that L. Feuerbach usually liked to appeal to Luther for his theory of the identity of divine with human essence, and therefore of God's becoming man which is really the manifestation of man become God?' (Barth *CD*, IV. 2, pp. 82f). The idealist theologians had set things up for Feuerbach with 'unparalleled naivete' (Barth *CD*, II. 1, p. 293).

Barth criticised Feuerbach for his fiction of species humanity – generalised man – and for failing to take seriously the individual before God's judgement – the individual who has sinned and must die (Barth 1972, p. 540). But Barth notoriously did not challenge – but rather specifically endorsed – Feuerbach's promethean assessment of religion as the expression of unregenerate anxiety, fear, sense of lack, sorrow and suffering, and rebellion against suffering as sent by God or the gods (Barth *CD* IV. 3, pp. 807f).

In fact Barth presupposed Feuerbach's anthropological reduction of religion. It played into Barth's hands, for according to Barth, religion is merely human striving towards and against God. Barth explicitly does not exclude the Christian religion from this assessment. All religion is unbelief; all religion is under judgement. No religion is true; a religion can only become true by an act of grace coming from without. A divine act of revelation and salvation can transform the status of religion – justifying and sanctifying it in despite of any intrinsic merits. There is an analogy – indeed a causal connection – between the free justification of sinners and the redemption of religion. 'Like justified man religion is a creature of grace' (Barth *CD*, II. 1, pp. 325ff). Barth works, therefore, with a distinction between Christian and non-Christian faith, justified and unjustified religion, divine revelation and human projection. This raises the problem of whether this is empirically discernible – can we tell the difference? – or whether it is merely a conceptual distinction, a paper doctrine, an arbitrary value judgement based on prejudice.

Barth claims that the modern world has rejected Christianity in its specific theological form and replaced it with mere religion. 'Religion exists. Religion is possible and necessary. But it is man who is the beginning, the middle and the end of religion – man and man alone' (Barth 1972, p. 536). This adoption of Feuerbach by Barth is the precarious alliance that underlies Barth's distinctive theology of revelation and remains its Achilles' heel in an age when constructive dialogue between the religions of the world appears imperative. Barth supped with the devil in the person of Feuerbach, and failed to use a long enough spoon.

Pannenberg has returned on several occasions to this problem of Barth's use of Feuerbach. In his *Systematic Theology I* Pannenberg argues that Barth's acceptance of Feuerbach's analysis for all forms of religion other than Christian revelation, faith and theology is implausible. All manifestations of religion have too much in common. For Pannenberg, Barth's dichotomy of justified and unjustified religion is not empirically discernible – it is arbitrary. 'The genetic connections and structural similarities between the history of biblical religion and its continuation in Christianity up to modern Christian proclamation and theology on the one side, and non-Christian religions on the other, are much too close for such a strategy to work' (Pannenberg 1992, p. 105).

However, Pannenberg makes what I regard as a more serious charge in the much earlier essay on atheism in *Basic Questions in Theology II*. Pannenberg asks whether Barth's approach is not in fact 'merely a case of withdrawing from controversy with Feuerbach and his disciples' and carrying on as if nothing had happened. Barth proposes a 'senseless renunciation of all critical discussion, and thus an act of spiritual capitulation to Feuerbach'. Christian theology cannot 'afford to surrender the whole field of religions to the Feuerbachian critique without endangering the truth of the

Christian faith itself and its speech about God'. Pannenberg recalls us to theological responsibility and sanity when he insists that 'the struggle over the concept of God has to be conducted indeed in the fields of philosophy, the sciences of religion, and anthropology. If Feuerbach should prove right in these fields, then the proof of atheism for which he strove would in fact be accomplished' (Pannenberg 1971, pp. 189f).

Feuerbach's thesis is simplicity itself – an irrefutable intuition: 'consciousness of God is self-consciousness, knowledge of God is self-knowledge' (Feuerbach 1957, p. 12). The paradox on which the plausibility of Feuerbach's claim pivots lies is the radical notion of a consciousness of which we are not conscious, a knowledge of which we have no knowledge – that is, of course, until Feuerbach comes along and informs us. We shall come in due course to the question of the truth of the reductionalist doctrine of projection, and I do not wish to give the impression at this stage that it is to be dismissed out of hand. But it is appropriate now to plant the seed of doubt and indicate that it is possible to call Feuerbach's logical bluff by citing (from Küng 1980, p. 210) the remarks of E. von Hartmann: 'It is quite true that nothing exists merely because we wish it, but it is not true that something cannot exist if we wish it. Feuerbach's whole critique of religion and the proof of his atheism, however, rest on this single argument, on a logical fallacy.'

From Feuerbach to Marx

Feuerbach's anthropological reduction of religion was a brilliant speculative intuition, arrived at by standing Hegelian principles on their head and so reversing Hegel's view of the relation of thought to being. For Hegel there is a unity, an identity of thought and being, so that true thought – and this, for Hegel, of course was never more definitively expressed than in his own system – is a revelation of the nature of being, an epiphany of ultimate reality. This can be said because ultimate reality is mind, reason or idea.

Feuerbach denies this and reverses the priority. As he put it in his *Preliminary Theses for the Reform of Philosophy*: 'The true relationship of thought to being is this: being is the subject, thought the predicate. Thought arises from being –

being does not arise from thought' (McLellan 1976, p. 68). Now, for Feuerbach, being – while certainly conceived naturalistically and materialistically – is fundamentally human existence under the aspect of the species' struggle for survival against a hostile or indifferent nature. Feuerbach lacks a sense of human existence as an artefact produced by human industry. He still retains a somewhat romantic and ethereal notion of human being – he has not finally cast off the trappings of Hegelian idealism. Marx would radically transform the concept of being, precisely by way of critique of Feuerbach, redescribing it as a socio-economic product.

3
Critique of Heaven and Earth:
Karl Marx

Every need to which reality denies satisfaction compels to belief.
(GOETHE, *Elective Affinities*, p. 298)

Biographical Background (1818–1883)

The first thing that must be said about Marx is that he was a man of faith. His inheritance was Jewish faith. His student commitment was to Christian and Lutheran faith. His adoption of Hegelianism had all the marks of religious conversion. The faith of his later years was dialectical materialism and its revolutionary programme. Marx gave his chief characteristic as single-mindedness (McLellan 1976, p. 457). Though the content of his faith changed from sacred to secular, he always demanded a conviction that would give a meaning to history and motivate him in his work for a greater cause (cf. Kee, p. 11).

As Marx's biographer, David McLellan, has commented, it would be difficult to find anyone who had a more thoroughly Jewish ancestry than Karl Marx. Almost all the rabbis of Trier where Marx grew up were ancestors of his on his father's side. His mother Henrietta was equally steeped in the rabbinic tradition and may well have kept Jewish customs alive in the home. Marx's father Heinrich, however, had broken with his family and made a diplomatic conversion to Protestantism (a small minority in the city). He remained a theist – or at least a deist, being described as a 'Protestant à la Lessing'. He recommended to Marx 'the faith of Newton, Locke and Leibniz' (McLellan 1976, pp. 2–6).

Marx's essays for his school-leaving examination evince great religious fervour. They reflect a pietistic faith in which union with Christ is vital and results in self-sacrificial service for the brethren. But they are definitely post-Enlightenment in their ethos. Christianity offers the possibility of the full moral development of humanity. Although there is a warmth about references to the person of Christ as redeemer, the conception of God at this stage is distant, colourless and somewhat deistic. God and nature are interchangeable (Kee, pp. 4ff; McLellan 1976, pp. 10ff). The essays are reminiscent of Schleiermacher's *Soliloquies*.

The transition in Marx's thinking to hostility towards religion is obscure. Did his captivation by the Romantics – taught to him by his future father-in-law Baron von Westphalen – liberate him from his childhood faith? At any rate, by the time of his doctoral dissertation Marx was making his own the defiance of Prometheus against the gods: 'In one word, I hate all gods.' This, he writes, is the profession, the slogan of philosophy against all gods in heaven and earth 'who do not recognise man's self-consciousness as the highest divinity'. And, in an apparent echo of the first commandment, Marx adds: 'There shall be none other beside it' (Marx 1972, p. 13).

It was said of the Young Hegelians (by Georg Jung): 'If Marx, Bruno Bauer and Feuerbach come together to found a theological-philosophical review, God would do well to surround himself with all his angels . . . for these three will certainly drive him out of his heaven.' For Marx, added this observer, 'The Christian religion is one of the most immoral there is' (McLellan 1976, p. 42). This judgement could at any rate appeal to Marx's slightly later opinion that 'the social principles of Christianity preach cowardice, self-abasement, resignation, submission and humility – in short all the characteristics of the *canaille* . . . The social principles of Christianity are sneaking and hypocritical' (p. 174).

Marx's Critique of Religion

No coherent or even consistent theory of religion is to be found in Marx's writings. Marx's comments on religion are scattered through various works and when brought together they hardly comprise a definitive position. As John Plamenatz has written in this connection: 'Marx and Engels were not careful thinkers . . . neither of them produced anything that could be called even a sketch for a theory of religion' (Plamenatz, p. 227). Unlike Feuerbach before them or Nietzsche and Freud after them, they do not attempt to explain how religious ideas and practices arose: they are interested only in their social function (ibid.).

Marx has a twofold analysis of religion. Primarily, religion is one of the forms of alienated life under capitalism, along with bourgeois morality, the state, law and forms of artistic expression. It is a fantasy, an illusion, of alienated humanity. The theory of religion as alienation is not original or distinctive to Marx, having been developed by Hegel and elaborated by Feuerbach in his distinctive sense. Secondarily (though this sense is more prominent in Engels), religion is typically the ideology of a particular class. As an ideology, it is of course a distortion, a form of false consciousness, and as such serves the interests of the dominant class, legitimating the oppression of the proletariat. In both respects – as fantasy and as ideology – religion has a narcotic value. As Plamenatz writes of Marx and Engels: 'At the root of religion as they conceive it, lie anxiety and diffidence and the sense of living in a hostile world; and the hopes it inspires serve above all to allay or to disguise these feelings. In this sense, it is always, even in its primitive forms, an opiate' (Plamenatz, p. 237).

Marx's disconnected, rhetorical and ambiguous remarks on religion leave several questions unanswered. Have all religions (even in societies without the kinds of division of labour that, according to Marx, produce alienation) been expressions of alienation? Have all religions (even in precapitalist societies without an economic class-structure) been class ideologies? Of which class is religion the class ideology – the oppressor or the oppressed? Does religion have one function for the oppressor – to legitimate its privileges – and another function for the oppressed – to reconcile it to its fate? These tantalising questions enable Plamenatz to claim that what Marx and Engels actually say is not sufficient to justify attributing to them the assumption that all forms of religion without exception are expressions of alienation and/ or class ideology (Plamenatz, pp. 207, 238, 243). But the virulent hostility of Marx himself, to all gods – which we have just observed – seems to rule out this milder interpretation.

There are, it seems, no grounds for hoping that Marx might have tolerated some forms of religion, perhaps in a future classless society, as benign.

Hegel had held that all religion is a form of self-externalis-ation or projection and is therefore normally a symptom of human alienation. It gives symbolic expression – its doctrines are not literally true – to the human sense of who we are, of our metaphysical identity, so to speak. Humanity attributes to a source beyond itself qualities that are essentially human, because humanity has not yet arrived at a true and just under-standing of itself and the world. But, for Hegel, not all religions express symbolically a sense of inadequacy, limi-tation or oppression; like Nietzsche later on, Hegel saw ancient Greek religion as an expression of confidence and harmony in the world. So, while all religion, for Hegel, is a form of self-externalisation, it is not all equally an expression of alienation. Judaism and Christianity represent the ultimate stage of self-estrangement when projections are elaborated into a sophisticated and advanced symbolic representation of the essence of humanity as spirit – and are therefore on the verge of overcoming it. So Christianity particularly expresses both humanity's alienated condition and the overcoming or transcending of it – but since it does this only figuratively it still contains illusion. Hegel's metaphysic shows absolute spirit coming to a realisation of itself through the evolution of human thought, including religion. The world is a predi-cate of mind. Feuerbach merely reverses this, making mind a predicate, product or projection of the natural world and the deep instinctive urge of the human species for survival, suc-cess and gratification (cf. Plamenatz, pp. 229ff).

If Feuerbach stands Hegel on his head, Marx turns them both inside out. While Marx's early writings reveal an accept-ance of the fundamental presupposition of the Feuerbachian critique – that humanity is the maker of religion and worships its own heavenly projection – the later *German Ideology* and *Theses on Feuerbach* present Marx's distinctive theory of religion as ideology. Here he goes beyond Feuerbach, who held to an essential human nature that was innately religious, to claim that religion and all other forms of ideology – cul-tural expressions and structures that gave meaning and legi-timation to an unjust society – were merely reflections of prevailing social conditions. The sixth thesis strikes the key-note: 'Feuerbach resolves the religious essence into the *human* essence. But the human essence is no abstraction inherent in each single individual. In its reality it is the ensemble of social relations'(Marx & Engels, pp. 665f).

If Feuerbach had reduced the transcendent to the level of consciousness, Marx reduced consciousness to social, indeed material conditions. 'Religion has no content of its own,' Marx wrote in connection with the thought of the Young Hegelians, 'and lives not from heaven but from earth, and falls of itself with the dissolution of the inverted reality whose theory it is' (McLellan 1987, p.10). As Marx and Engels put it in *The German Ideology*, the Young Hegelians (and this includes Feuerbach) regard 'conceptions, thoughts, ideas, in fact all the products of consciousness, to which they attribute an independent existence, as the real chains of men' – and these were precisely the notions that 'the Old Hegelians' regarded as 'the true bonds of human society' (p. 30). But true liberation 'is a historical and not a mental act and it is brought about by historical conditions' (p. 56). While all forms of ideology – morality, religion, metaphysics, law, etc. – are the product of the particular life-processes of individuals, they are not produced in the way these individuals imagine: they are not produced by people as they moralise, theologise, theorise, but 'as they operate, produce materially and hence as they work under definite material limits, presuppositions and conditions independent of their will' (p. 37). In other words, 'life is not determined by consciousness but consciousness by life' (p. 38). This approach 'does not explain practice from the idea but explains the formation of ideas from material practice' (p. 50). Ideology is defined by its turning the true relation of theory and practice, consciousness and material conditions upside down 'as in a *camera* obscura' – though this fact in itself is a product by the historical life-process, just as the inversion of objects on the retina is produced by the physical life-process (p. 37).

In this perspective, as Marx wrote at around this time in his introduction to his proposed *Critique of Hegel's Philosophy of Right* (1844), religion is merely an ideological reflex or echo of the conditions of a given life-process, 'inverted' in its attitude to the world because the conditions in which it thrives are inverted. 'Man makes religion, religion does not make man.' Religion is the expression of human alienation. 'But man is no abstract being squatting outside the world. Man is the world of man, the state, society.' Religion is the 'sigh of the oppressed creature, the feeling of a heartless world, and the soul of soulless circumstances ... the opium of the people ... illusory happiness', destined to fade away when oppressive conditions were removed. Religion is an evil because it is always the expression and legitimation (the 'halo' and 'spiritual aroma') of an unjust society. The struggle against religion is therefore a struggle against an oppressive system. Critique of religion is the beginning, the presupposition (*Voraussetzung*) of all critique (Marx 1972, pp. 115f). Marx does not entertain the possibility that there could be forms of religious expression that affirm human dignity, freedom and fulfilment (Harvey, p. 309). Religion was entirely attributable to empirical causes, without introducing the esoteric causality of the religious spirit itself. Therefore there was no need to distinguish between religion and superstition, or true and false religion. Belief in one god was as ridiculous as belief in many (McKown, p. 33). All religion made man a 'degraded, enslaved, rejected, contemptible being'. Nevertheless, this description of religion as a 'pain killer', 'constitutes the most gentle treatment Marx ever accorded religion' (McKown, p. 52).

Religion is both symptom and cause of human alienation. 'As long as man is imprisoned within religion,' wrote Marx in *On the Jewish Question*, 'he only knows how to objectify his essence by making it into an alien, imaginary being' (Marx 1972, p. 114). In this respect, Marx regards Christianity as 'the religion *par excellence*, the essence of religion, deified man' (p. 65). The task of philosophy, Marx proclaims, is to reveal 'self-alienation in all its unholy forms' and so expose the conditions which generate religion. 'The criticism of heaven is thus transformed into the criticism of earth, criticism of religion into the criticism of law, and the criticism of theology into the criticism of politics' (p. 116). The unmasking of religion is the converse of the protest against oppression: 'The criticism of religion ends with the doctrine that man is the highest being for man, hence with the categorical imperative to overthrow all conditions in which man is a degraded, enslaved, neglected, contemptible being' (cf. Bernstein, p. 41). However, religion, like all ideologies, cannot be dissolved by intellectual criticism alone, but 'only by the practical overthrow of the actual social relations which gave rise to this idealistic humbug' (Marx & Engels, p. 50; cf. p. 56). Then, as Marx stressed in his late work, religion will have no *raison d'être* and will wither away. As he wrote in *Capital*: 'The religious reflections of the real world can, in any case, vanish only when the practical relations of everyday life between man and man, and man and nature, generally present themselves to him in a transparent and rational form' (McLellan 1987, p. 31).

Erich Fromm entitled his 'encounter with the thought of Marx and Freud' *Beyond the Chains of Illusion*. For Marx, those chains were material ones; for Feuerbach they were mental ones; but for Freud they were anchored deep in the unconscious of the individual.

Reflection and Agenda

In the present climate, it is tempting to ignore the challenge that Marx presents to Christian theology. The Eastern European regimes that purported to be based on Marx's economic theories have collapsed. State socialism patently failed to bring freedom, equality and prosperity to its people. Marx's reputation and with it the influence of his thought as a whole has suffered eclipse. The political weakness of Marxism today is compounded for theology and religious studies by what even exponents of Marx admit to be the sporadic, unsystematic and unscholarly character of Marx's critique of religion. But to adopt that complacent view – that Marx no longer presents a threat to traditional unreconstructed versions of Christian theology – would be very shortsighted.

Marx has actually achieved a fundamental change in our perception of religion. After Marx it is not possible to regard religion, with its doctrines, its rituals and its power structures, naively. Marx has compelled us to view religion with suspicion. He has taken away its innocence. Of course he was not the first to do this. Before Marx was Feuerbach and both Feuerbach and Marx were heirs of the Enlightenment. The English deists, Hume, Gibbon and the French *philosophes* prepared the ground for the nineteenth-century reductionists by exposing the all-too-human aspect of institutional religion. They challenged the intolerance of ecclesiastical authority, the oppression of priestcraft, the corruption of texts and the stifling of free enquiry. As we have seen, the concept of projection was familiar to the eighteenth century, though its deep psychological dynamics were not understood. Feuerbach took the Enlightenment's critique of religion a stage further by reducing religion to a function of human consciousness. Religion was no longer the product of priestly conspiracy, but the inexorable projection of humanity alienated from itself. But it was Marx who showed that consciousness is a function of material conditions.

This was a third stage of the deconstruction of religion. The first was the Enlightenment's critique of the sacrosanct teachings and privileges of the Church in the name of reason. The second was Feuerbach's reduction of those teachings to functions of the alienated human consciousness. Then Marx claimed that human consciousness was actually the 'ensemble of social relations' grounded in economic conditions.

For Marx, religion does not descend from heaven; it is immersed in earthly, human, material fact. 'Man makes religion, religion does not make man.' Religion belongs to the ideological superstructure of society; it is the distorted shadow of its unjust material base, the product of false consciousness. The ideological character of religion, according to Marx, is threefold.

- First, it is a reified, idealised abstraction of reality, concealing the truth about society. It postulates a spurious wholeness, as in Hegel's 'The whole is the true.' It creates an illusion of a world that is in a state of harmony by reconciling conflicts of human interest at a theoretical, rather than at a practical level.
- Second, it serves a narcotic function, as the opium of the people, stilling the pain of their unjust situation by building up hopes of recompense hereafter. It does this most subtly by incorporating their cries of protest into its scheme, as expressions of hope deferred.
- Third, it is the ideology of the ruling class, employed to keep the proletariat in a position of weakness and

subservience. The dominant ideas of a society are the ideas sponsored and endorsed by the dominant group. This is its most sinister, oppressive ideological function.

It is not in the least evident to me that these three connected criticisms of religion are disposed of by pointing to the failure of economic systems that invoked the authority of Marx or by adducing the occasional, unsystematic and unrigorous nature of Marx's critique of religion. It is not so much his specific comments on religion that are so telling as his fundamental insight that religion is a human product, bearing all the marks of the socio-economic nexus, with all its inequalities and injustices, that produced it.

Marx has compelled us to see at the very least that the phenomena of religion – doctrines, rituals, authority structures – are distorted (Marx would say determined) by their socio-economic milieu. Doctrines have an ideological character that puts them on a par with economic, political, philosophical and other theories. Their substance is not derived exclusively (Marx would say, at all) from divine revelation; they are not transparent to a transcendent realm. They serve the non-theological interests, which are ultimately socio-economic, of those who frame them, elaborate them, inculcate them, celebrate them ritually, and enforce them. There is no belief or practice that is not ideological in the sense of being shaped (Marx would say produced) by impure ideological motives. Religion is actually an extreme case of ideological construction and distortion.

Where does this leave the truth of Christian faith? I want to argue that, rightly understood, Christian faith can welcome this Marxian critique and be purified and strengthened by it. A full analysis of the concept of ideology as found in Marx and developed by Mannheim and others, and with it the necessary argumentation as to how the constraints of ideology can be assimilated dialectically and thus ultimately transcended, must await a proposed sequel to this volume. But the following points may serve to indicate that Marx's method of ideological criticism is not necessarily fatal to vital Christian truth claims – even though it does radically subvert all distortions of the Gospel, all our failure to live out Christian truth, and all inflated claims of ecclesiastical authority.

Marx does not allow for the possibility of genuine divine revelation, however conceived, which enlightens the minds of its recipients to see through the blatant socio-economic motivations of institutional religion. The Scriptures of the Christian Church (not to mention those of other religions) provide impressive cumulative testimony to the phenomenon of human encounter with a transcendent realm, in the form of numinous experience, resulting in ethically powerful prophecy or proclamation.

He does not envisage that there could be forms of religion that are socially beneficent and therapeutic – that challenge the rich and powerful, and that inspire the poor and oppressed to transform their situation. The Liberation theologians of Latin America in particular, who owe much to Marx in terms of his analysis of class conflict, reject Marx's reductionist account of religion and instead find their inspiration for a socially subversive faith – one that refutes Marx's analysis – in the Exodus or the Magnificat.

Marx misses a vital dimension of Christianity: its innate ability to be continually reforming itself, to adapt in the light of new knowledge and changed circumstances. He neglects the apophatic tradition of theology, which continually subverts all human attempts to belittle, domesticate and idolise the transcendent. Marx would have no doubt been bewildered at the suggestion that the critique of Christianity belongs to the very essence of Christianity. It undermines his fundamental assumption about religion.

4
The Implausible Antichrist:
Friedrich Nietzsche

Friedrich Nietzsche is without a doubt the most lethal adversary of the Christian faith in modern times. What the emperor Nero was to the Christian martyrs of the first century, the philosopher Nietzsche is to Christian intellectuals of the twentieth. His onslaught against Christianity in, for example, *The Genealogy of Morals, The Antichrist,* and the fragmentary *The Will to Power,* is incisive, implacable, and devastating. His last work before the onset of madness, the autobiographical manifesto *Ecce Homo,* ends with the unambiguous challenge: 'Have I been understood? – *Dionysus against the Crucified . . .' (EH,* p. 134). Yet Christianity is not the only, or even the primary target of Nietzsche's polemic. He has all the forms of idealism – indeed, all expressions of noble aspiration – in his sights. 'Where *you* see ideal things,' he asserts, '*I* see – human, alas all too human things' (*EH,* p. 89). Nietzsche is a Midas in reverse: his touch turns all that is gold back into common things; he is the perverted alchemist who converts precious metal into base. Logic, language, philosophy and metaphysics – even reason itself – fall victim to his deconstructive approach and Christian theology is savaged in the process. Yet there is a sense in which the idea of God is the ultimate object of Nietzsche's enmity. As he wrote in the preface to *Human, All Too Human*: 'I myself do not believe that anyone has ever before looked into the world with an equally profound degree of suspicion and not merely as an occasional devil's advocate, but, to speak theologically, just as much as an enemy and indicter of God' (*HH,* p. 5).

For the secular postmodernists, as Milbank reminds us (Milbank, p. 278), Nietzsche is the master of baseless suspicion – an all consuming corrosive that, unlike the suspicion of Marx, Freud and the sociology of knowledge, rests on no foundationalist presuppositions but only on its own jaundiced vision – one that ultimately destroyed its protagonist. The Nietzsche who probes unsparingly human psychology and motivation with his scalpel of suspicion, is of course the progenitor of Foucault's method of 'genealogy' which retrieves 'the singularity of events', searching for them 'in the most unpromising places, in what we tend to feel is without history – in sentiments, love, conscience, instincts'. While Nietzsche himself is ambivalent about the significance to be accorded a knowledge of the origin of human beliefs, emotions, and institutions – sometimes, as we shall see, committing the genetic fallacy with a vengeance – Foucault himself intends to be more consistent, renouncing questions of evolution and teleology and opposing the search for origins (Foucault, pp. 76f). Nietzsche's essay on the philosophy of history (the second of his *Untimely Meditations*), which asserts that all present political regimes are founded on the crimes of past history, becomes the stimulus for Foucault's construal of history as a series of stratagems of power (Milbank, pp. 281f).

It is then not only Christian believers and theologians who have to grapple with Nietzsche, and who afterwards still have to be able to give a reason for the hope that is in them, but all who wish to take their stand on the values of reasoned discourse in epistemology, ethics, metaphysics and aesthetics – unless, like the deconstructionists, the anarchists of learning, they choose to throw in their lot with Nietzsche by an act of intellectual suicide, despairing of rhyme or reason in our common discourse; or, like the Christian fideists, they convince themselves that the Christian faith, as a conceptuality revealed vertically from above (as Barth put it), creates its own narrative world – one that is impervious to Nietzsche's acids. These non-realist theologians accept his conclusions about ethics, metaphysics and non-Christian religions – but that only highlights for them the fact that the Christian faith is *sui generis*. They enrol Nietzsche as an ally against the critics and rivals of Christian belief, hoisting them with their own petard. They accept with equanimity his devastating critique of the Church as an historical phenomenon: they can afford to be patronisingly dismissive of Christendom, for they are naturally among the free-floating Christian intelligentsia who extol the community of faith in the abstract while taking care not to soil their hands by getting involved in the hard grind of being a Christian in the institutional Church.

In reading Nietzsche – an incomparable intellectual experience – we need to make allowance for his extreme language and provocative postures. As Schacht says, his style is 'often excessively metaphorical, unnecessarily hyperbolical, overly combative and provocative to a fault' (Schacht, p. 59). By the time of his impending madness Nietzsche's posturing had become second nature and fantasy had become reality to him. 'I no longer speak with words but with lightning bolts,' he proclaims in *Ecce Homo*. 'I am not a man I am dynamite' (*EH*, pp. 87, 126).

However excessive Nietzsche's style may often be, at its best it is marked by a limpid grace and lyrical simplicity. Near the beginning of his authorial career, Nietzsche remarks that simplicity of style has always been the mark of genius, which expresses itself simply, naturally, and with naivety. But the author of genius is also a virtuoso, dominating his material creatively: 'his abundant power plays with his material even when it is difficult and dangerous. Stiff and timid steps will get no one along unfamiliar paths littered with a thousand abysses: the genius, however, runs nimbly along such paths with daring or elegant strides and disdains cautiously to measure his steps' (*UM*, p. 46).

Nietzsche's argument is like his language. It is not discursive, orderly and logical, but intuitive, spontaneous and sporadic. His thought is not systematic, but occasional, related to issues that incur his analysis. We look in vain, therefore, for complete consistency in Nietzsche's writings. Where contradictory statements appear, they are not successive and chronological but simultaneous. Nevertheless, a coherent position is achieved by Nietzsche within which there is obvious development. It is his views on human nature (anthropology), the tasks of philosophy, the possibility of metaphysics, the grounds of religion and ethics and specifically of Christianity that concern us. Within each area we shall cover Nietzsche's thought in broadly chronological order.

Biographical Background (1844–1900)

Nietzsche's father and grandfather were both Lutheran pastors. His father died when Nietzsche was five and he grew up in a household of gently pious women. Nietzsche came to associate Christianity with what was soft, enervating, feeble and neurotic. This claustrophobic domestic setting may well have contributed to the self-absorption, virtually narcissism, that characterised Nietzsche from an early age. His bereavement, at an age when his feelings towards his father would be at their most Oedipally ambiguous, left a vacuum which Nietzsche tried to fill with a succession of father-figures – most notably Schopenhauer and Wagner – who were first idolised and then overcome.

As a boy, Nietzsche was outstanding for his piety. He could quote Bible passages and hymns and was nicknamed 'little pastor' by his fellow schoolboys. Nietzsche's confirmation was by all accounts a deeply moving experience. Paul Deussner recalled:

> When the candidates for confirmation went in twos to the altar, where they knelt to receive their consecration, Nietzsche also knelt ... I remember well the sense of holiness and detachment from the world that filled us during the weeks before and after confirmation. We would have been quite prepared there and then to die in order to be with Christ, and all our thinking, feeling and activity was resplendent with a more than earthly serenity. (Küng 1980, p. 353)

There is an early poem that expresses a emotional dedication comparable to the prayers of the mystics such as St John of the Cross:

> Thou has called:
> Lord I hurry
> And tarry
> At the steps of thy throne.

> Burning with love
> Thy gaze so heartily
> Painfully
> Shines into my heart:
> Lord, I come.
>   (O'Flaherty, Sellner and Helm, p. 92)

In 1881 he recalled to Overbeck, the Church historian who had turned against Christianity himself, 'As for my attitude to Christianity, there is one thing you will surely believe: in my heart I have never really opposed it, and from my childhood days I frequently made a great inward effort towards its ideals, though in the last years I always came up against sheer impossibility' (Stern, p. 15).

It was aged 20, at the end of his first semester at Bonn where he was studying philology and theology, that he read D. F. Strauss's *Lebens Jesu* and lost his faith. He returned home for Easter and announced to his distraught mother and sister that he no longer believed in God, could not make his communion on Easter Day, and intended to give up the theological component of his studies (Pletsch, pp. 67–9).

Moving to the university of Leipzig to pursue pure philology, Nietzsche took lodgings over a bookshop and discovered there in 1865 Schopenhauer's *The World as Will and Representation*. Devouring it avidly, Nietzsche experienced something akin to a religious conversion, a moral and spiritual rebirth, accompanied by a powerful sense of philosophical vocation that would consort uneasily with his philological career until at the age of 45 Nietzsche retired from the chair at Basle that he had so brilliantly acquired at the age of 24.

Nietzsche recalled in the essay 'Schopenhauer as Educator' that it was while he was in a state of 'need, distress and desire' that he discovered Schopenhauer. He found that the philosopher spoke to him through his writings like a father to his son. It was the personal, paternal qualities of honesty, steadfastness and cheerfulness, rather than the metaphysical system, that appealed to Nietzsche. As his own sense of himself as a neglected philosophical genius developed, Nietzsche came to see Schopenhauer as a model of the unheeded prophet who paid the price of telling the truth (*UM*, pp. 133–8, 152). In working out his own destiny as the neglected genius, Nietzsche came to believe that Schopenhauer had had to overcome three adversaries: his contemporaries (who ignored him), his mentors (especially Kant) and finally himself (in order to become a 'redemptive man') (Pletsch, p. 178). Consequently, Nietzsche resolved to write only of his own 'overcomings' (*HH*, p. 209: II. Preface). He came to regard Schopenhauer as his first and only educator (ibid.)

However, Nietzsche owed an abiding debt to Schopenhauer's philosophy. This freelance philosopher published his first book in 1813 at the age of 25. His *magnum opus*, successively revised and expanded throughout his life, *The World as Will and Representation* appeared in 1819 when its author was merely 31. Schopenhauer died in 1860, five years before Nietzsche read him. Nietzsche was influenced by Schopenhauer in his metaphysics and his epistemology but parted company from him in his ethics. Schopenhauer asserted the metaphysical priority of Will. The world that we experience in perception is the objectified representation of a ruthlessly powerful cosmic force, the Will to Live, a blind incessant impulse generating endless striving. The noumenal Will, is unknowable and eternal. The world we inhabit is a veil of illusion, constructed by our own perceptions, and marked by futility, violence and pain. Desire is also a form of pain. We may escape its pangs temporarily through aesthetic contemplation but permanently only by an almost unattainable act of abnegation that annihilates the self along with its world.

Nietzsche retains the metaphysical priority of Will – not, however, the Will to Live, but the Will to Power. He insists on the illusoriness and ephemerality of the world, as does Schopenhauer, but in a radical reversal of his mentor's conclusions, Nietzsche affirms the change, flux and transitoriness – the continual becoming – of the cosmic process. And, instead of teaching escape from it through artistic contemplation and an ultimate selfless Nirvana, Nietzsche plunges into the maelstrom in the Dionysan frenzy of artistic creation, a state of intoxication with the powers of the Will working through the surrendered soul of the genius.

The tragedy of Nietzsche's life is that his early narcissism came full circle. The impulses of his own heart became the sole object of artistic creativity. And the self-surrender that he made was to no 'power, not ourselves, that makes for righteousness', but to his own perverted will that, having stifled all feelings of compassion and pity, would not allow him to let up on himself. It is not necessary to invoke syphilis to account for Nietzsche's inspiration and self-destruction. The logic of his creed is explanation enough.

Nietzsche's Basic Worldview

A glance at Nietzsche's basic worldview sets the scene for more detailed consideration of his views on philosophy and theology. His worldview comprises what we might call his cosmology and his anthropology – his vision of nature and of human life. Let us take the latter first.

Nietzsche's anthropology is a thoroughly cynical and jaundiced one, an uncompromising picture of blind selfish desire working its remorseless will in the fate of the human species. In his early essay 'On Truth and Falsity in their Ultramoral Sense' (1873), Nietzsche portrayed the human mind as wretched, shadowy, transitory and purposeless. Deception is the particular character of the intellect and it serves the preservation of the individual. Nietzsche outdoes Machiavelli and Hobbes in designating human relations as one great act of dissimulation, marked by deception, flattery, falsehood, fraud, slander, display, pretentiousness and disguise – all fluttering around the flame of vanity. Nature has thrown away the key to the secrets of our being – and 'woe to the fateful curiosity which might be able for a moment to look . . . through a crevice in the chamber of consciousness, and discover that man, indifferent to his own ignorance, is resting on the pitiless, the greedy, the insatiable, the murderous, and, as it were, hanging in dreams on the back of a tiger' (Nietzsche *TF*, pp. 173–6). From the same early period, the essay on Schopenhauer exposes humanity as a beast of prey driven by the futility of desire:

> The tremendous coming and going of men on the great wilderness of the earth, their founding of cities and states, their wars, their restless assembling and scattering again, their confused mingling, mutual imitation, mutual outwitting and downtreading, their wailing in distress,

their howls of joy in victory – all this is a continuation of animality. (*UM*, p. 158)

Yet the essence of humanity transcends nature, and the goal of humanity's journey – 'it's great sorrowful way through the desert of the past' (*HH*, p. 135) – stands high above us. The unconscious purpose of nature is to produce philosophers, artists and saints, those who can bring to blind humanity the enlightenment of self-knowledge (*UM*, pp. 159ff). This is the ultimate reason why, from *Human All too Human* onwards, Nietzsche rejects the emotion of pity – either for oneself or for others. In spite of – or rather because of – the pervasiveness of pain, pity, which would deflect nature from its (blind) purpose, is to be resisted. Zarathustra himself is philosopher, artist and saint, but he also prefigures the super-man of Nietzsche's later writings, whose naked will to power eclipses the gentler aspirations of the three redemptive figures of the early Nietzsche. In *The Gay Science/The Joyful Wisdom*, Nietzsche asserts that the essence of humanity is the conservation of the species, through a process governed by inexorable instinct. This overriding claim of group survival leads Nietzsche to designate morality as 'the herd instinct in the individual' (*JW*, pp. 31, 161: paras 1, 116). Reason is a mere epiphenomenon and disguises the origin of culture in instinct and unreason. 'All things that live long are gradually so saturated with reason that their origin in unreason thereby becomes improbable' (*D*, p. 9: para. 1). Even logic originated in instinct (*JW*, p. 157: para. 110). Nietzsche speculates on the price, in blood and horror, that humanity has had to pay for reason, seriousness and control of the emotions – 'those grand human prerogatives and cultural showpieces' (*GM*, p. 194). This unnatural restraint, necessary for survival, found an outlet for repressed instinct in sadism and masochism, guilt and punishment, the foundation of religion:

> Man, with his need for self-torture, his sublimated cruelty resulting from the cooping up of his animal nature within a polity, invented bad conscience in order to hurt himself, after the blocking of the more natural outlet of his cruelty. Then this guilt-ridden man seized upon religion in order to exacerbate his self-torment to

the utmost. The thought of being in God's debt became the last instrument of torture. (*GM*, pp. 225f)

Here, Nietzsche continues, we see an insanity of the will without parallel: 'man's will to find himself guilty, and unredeemably so; his will to believe that he might be punished to all eternity without even expunging his guilt . . . What a mad, unhappy animal is man!' (p. 226).

Nietzsche's cosmology – his metaphysical worldview – undergirds this sombre anthropology. Nietzsche's metaphysic of ultimate reality is a form of dynamic materialism. The world is governed by absolute necessity driven by the cosmic will to power. Nietzsche's is not a mechanical materialism, based on lawlike causality, but a dynamic one in which an apparently random and merciless pattern of physical constituents serves a blind, unconscious cosmic purpose. Nietzsche's denial of ethical norms and moral responsibility is an inference from his view of nature and history as a succession of meaningless incidents.

Nietzsche's first book, the notorious *The Birth of Tragedy* (1871), invoked a primal unity of suffering as the sole foundation of the world (*BT*, pp. 25f). This vision comes to focus in *The Gay Science* where Nietzsche insists that 'the general character of the world . . . is to all eternity chaos; not by the absence of necessity, but in the sense of the absence of order, structure, form, beauty, wisdom.' There are no laws in nature, only necessities, and therefore there is no chance either. Notions of natural law and an orderly cosmos are relics of religious belief, the shadow of God (*JW*, p. 152: para. 109).

In *The Birth of Tragedy*, Nietzsche expounds his celebrated polarity of the Dionysan and the Apollonian. The Dionysan pertains to the nature of reality as generative, creative and chaotic – to which we open ourselves in passion and frenzy. The Apollonian pertains to the bearable appearance that we give to reality in art and especially tragic drama which has the power to enchant the terrible events portrayed, bringing delight and redemption through the power of illusion (*BT*, p. 61). At this stage, Nietzsche believes that only as an aesthetic phenomenon can the world be ultimately justified (pp. 8, 32). Therefore art, not morality, is the proper metaphysical task for humanity (pp. 7, 13). There is a 'metaphysical consolation' in submitting to nature, 'the Primal Mother, eternally creative, eternally impelling into life, eternally drawing satisfaction from the ceaseless flux of phenomena' (p. 80). Thus we reconcile ourselves to the fact that we humans are mere projections of the creative power (p. 25).

Nietzsche's late concept of the eternal return is a reaffirmation and reinforcement of this early insight. It expresses unqualified reconciliation to the world in its nature as will. The deep love and hunger for eternity in *Zarathustra* part 3 is fulfilled in 'the ring of rings – the Ring of Recurrence'. As Nietzsche claims in *Ecce Homo*, the idea of eternal recurrence is 'the highest formula of affirmation that can possibly be attained' (*EH*, p. 99).

Nietzsche on Philosophy

Nietzsche's views on philosophy will lead us to his stance on religion. The overwhelming impression received from reading Nietzsche is his hostility to metaphysics. But he does not discard metaphysics – he constantly engages in it, as we have just seen in discussing his worldview or cosmology. It is traditional, Western metaphysics that incurs Nietzsche's scorn and contempt. He castigates it for its idealism, dualism and intellectualism. For 'metaphysics' in Nietzsche we should read 'metaphysics as we have known it'. Even then Nietzsche still feels its lure – especially, he admits, when listening to Beethoven's Ninth Symphony (*HH*, p. 82)! This hostility to traditional philosophy does not mean that Nietzsche has a modern analytical understanding of philosophy – as engaging in the analysis of statements, meanings or forms of life. Though Nietzsche is second to none in his powers of analysis, he does not rest with a notion of philosophy that, like Wittgenstein's, 'leaves everything as it is'. As Schacht asserts, Nietzsche has an interventionist, legislative view of the philosopher. The philosopher à la Nietzsche is the creator of values, a commander and law-giver, who brings about a 'revaluation of all values'. Philosophy, on this understanding is the most spiritual form of the will to power (*BGE*, pp. 111f, 122f: paras 204, 211).

Traditional philosophers are a corrupt breed, devoid of

intellectual integrity. Their pretensions to eternal truth conceal a frankly autobiographical method: their great systems are simply 'memoirs' (*BGE*, p. 19: para. 6). They merely followed their prejudices and a suspicious deconstruction of their thought exposes ulterior motives. 'Every philosophy also *conceals* a philosophy; every opinion is also a hiding place, every word also a mask' (*BGE*, p. 197: para. 289). Philosophers construct conceptual mummies, attempting to preserve timeless truths (*TI*, p. 35: para. 1). But for Nietzsche, as he asserted in the Foreword to *Ecce Homo*, invoking his favourite imagery for landscapes of the mind, philosophy means choosing to inhabit the realms of ice and mountain peaks, 'a seeking after everything strange and questionable in existence, all that has hitherto been excommunicated by morality . . . wandering in the forbidden' (*EH*, p. 34). In the same book, Nietzsche describes philosophy as explosive material, putting everything in danger – a far cry from Kant and other 'academic ruminants' (unfair to Kant whose philosophy was explosive enough in its refutation of naive realism and the received proofs for the existence of God) (*EH*, p. 88).

Philosophy has been a catalogue of errors ('the science that treats of the fundamental errors of mankind . . . as though they were fundamental truths': *HH*, p. 22: I. 18) because the philosophers have been biased by a deep prejudice against becoming – against change, flux and process; against appearance, decay, suffering and pain; against the body, the senses and the sensual; against the irrational, purposeless and fateful – against life itself (*WP*, I, p. 327: para. 407). Philosophers have blindly trusted concepts while they have mistrusted the senses. To the extent that 'our prejudice in favour of reason compels us to posit unity, identity, duration, substance, cause, materiality, being,' we are inevitably immersed in error (*TI*, p. 37: para. 5). Against this Nietzsche sets a great Dionysan 'affirmation of transitoriness *and destruction* . . . affirmation of antithesis and war, *becoming* with a radical rejection even of the concept "*being*" ', an elemental '*joy even in destruction*' (*EH*, pp. 81, 111).

Nietzsche believes that in exposing the origins of metaphysics, including religious beliefs, in personal predilections and prejudices, he has refuted them. One of his fuller statements comes in *Human All Too Human*:

All that has begotten these assumptions is passion, error and self-deception; the worst of all methods of acquiring knowledge, not the best of all, have taught belief in them. When one has disclosed these methods as the foundation of all extant religions and metaphysical systems, one has refuted them! (*HH*, p. 15: I. 9)

This statement plunges Nietzsche straight into the genetic fallacy – judging the truth or error of a proposition merely by locating its source rather than on its intellectual merits. He proceeds to compound this mistake by asserting that metaphysical ideas are now just ideas floating about in the intellectual environment; we can play about with them if we like, but they have no serious claim to be considered cognitive – they bear no relation to reality for they originate in prejudice, fantasy and ignorance:

As soon as the origin of religion, art and morality is so described that it can be perfectly understood without the postulation of *metaphysical interference* at the commencement or in the course of their progress, the greater part of our interest . . . ceases to exist. For with religion, art and morality we do not touch upon the 'nature of the world in itself'; we are in the realm of ideas, no 'intuition' can take us any further. The question of how our conception of the world could differ so widely from the disclosed nature of the world will with perfect equanimity be relinquished to the physiology and history of the evolution of organisms and concepts. (*HH*, p. 16: I. 10)

We shall now see this approach applied to theology and ethics.

Nietzsche's Critique of Religion and Ethics

Nietzsche lays it down that no religion has ever contained any truth (*HH*, p. 62: I. 110). His onslaught on religion and ethics is fuelled by righteous indignation against their false pretensions to legislate for truth. There is therefore a paradox that Nietzsche's attack on ethics is motivated by ethical concern and his crusade against religion is fired by a sense of justice and compassion. For him 'all religions are at bottom systems of cruelty' in which irrational feelings of guilt (which Nietzsche explains as originating in notions of debt and obligation in a commodity culture) are manipulated by the priests 'the virtuosos of guilt'. Religion originates in a desire to punish oneself. He holds that human nature is basically sado-masochistic: 'To behold suffering gives pleasure, but to cause another to suffer affords an even greater pleasure' (*GM*, pp. 192, 198). Humans find a perverse satisfaction in inflicting pain upon themselves and religion is the ultimate expression of this (*GM*, pp. 225f). Nietzsche laments the human urge to self-destruction:

> In such psychological cruelty we see an insanity of the *will* that is without parallel: man's will to find himself guilty, and unredeemably so; his will to believe that he might be punished to all eternity without even expunging his guilt; his will to poison the very foundation of things in the problem of guilt and punishment . . . What a mad unhappy animal is man! (*GM*, p. 226)

Elsewhere Nietzsche attributes religion to a lack, not an excess of will. It is the weak-willed who cling to belief, 'for the will as emotion of command, is the distinguishing characteristic of sovereignty and power. That is to say, the less a person knows how to command, the more urgent is his desire for one who commands, who commands strongly' – whether that be God, dogma, the priest-confessor, or the political equivalent, the leader, the prince among men. Thus religion originates in an 'extraordinary *malady of the will*' (*JW*, p. 286: para. 347). In both aetiologies Nietzsche attributes religion to a disorder of the will.

By locating all true value in God, religion empties humanity and the world of value. Religion indulges in the 'forbidden generosity', for there is not enough love and goodness in the world for us to give any of it away to imaginary things (*HH*, p. 69: I. 129). Similarly, Nietzsche holds that spirituality can only be attained at the expense of bodily vitality: 'Wherever the teaching of *pure spirituality* has ruled, it has destroyed nervous energy with its excesses: it has taught deprecation, neglect or tormenting of the body.' Men blamed the poor body for the powerful forbidden drives that filled them, and sublimated these into ecstasy 'and other precursors of madness' which unfit us for ordinary life (*D*, pp. 27, 32f: paras 39, 60). It is this deficit of human value in religion that Nietzsche has in mind when he asserts that by denying God we redeem the world (*TI*, p. 54).

Because religious belief meets a psychological need it is virtually irrefutable in the individual. 'For such is man: a theological dogma may be refuted to him a thousand times,' but if it fills a need its truth will remain intact (*JW*, p. 285: para. 387). Faith is not rational but an 'acquired habituation to spiritual principles without reasons' (*HH*, p. 109: I. 226). Therefore Nietzsche sees no need to attempt a rational refutation of Christianity, for example by demolishing the traditional theistic proofs. It is enough to show the provenance of religious belief in irrationality: 'In former times, one sought to prove that there is no God – today one indicates how the belief that there is a God could *arise* and how this belief acquired its weight and importance: a counter-proof that there is no God thereby becomes superfluous' (*D*, p. 54: para. 95). Attacking arguments always left the possibility of better ones being put forward, for 'in those days atheists did not know how to make a clean sweep' (ibid.). For Nietzsche, therefore, religious belief is intuitive, irrational and arbitrary. But there is a profound irony here, for Nietzsche is not ashamed to confess that his atheism is equally intuitive and unfounded on reasoned argument: 'I have absolutely no knowledge of atheism as an outcome of reasoning . . . with me it is obvious by instinct' (*EH*, p. 51).

The founders of the great religions have been those individuals who were most given up to these overwhelming irrational feelings: they have a thirst for things that are contrary to reason, and therefore have never stopped to examine their intuitions in the light of intellect or conscience (*JW*, p. 248: para. 319). Nietzsche typically abuses saints and prophets as 'holy epileptics' and 'moral cretins'. It was easy for those who already held a concept of divine revelation to explain their overwhelming feelings as a revelation from God for 'how should a man be the originator of such great joy!' (*D*, pp. 37f: para. 62).

Nietzsche has an original and subtle thesis to explain the impending collapse of religion and Christianity (as he sees it). It is the purity of the Christian impulse for truth that itself will conquer Christianity. Christian morality, which probes the conscience and uncovers every hiding place for sin, Christian veracity which exposes every deception in the light of God, the confessional subtlety of the Christian conscience, the desire for intellectual integrity at any price – these are the ultimate sources of the overthrow of belief in God. It is 'Europe's longest and bravest self-conquest' (*JW*, p. 308: para. 357). The European consciousness, profoundly informed by Christianity and its love of the truth, has turned against itself; the better nature of Christianity has prevailed against Christendom. As Nietzsche put it in *The Genealogy of Morals*:

> All great things perish of their own accord, by an act of self-cancellation; so the law of life decrees ... Thus Christianity as dogma perished by its own ethics, and in the same way Christianity as ethics must perish; we are standing on the threshold of this event. After drawing a whole series of conclusions, Christian truthfulness must now draw its strongest conclusion, the one by which it shall do away with itself. This will be accomplished by Christianity's asking itself, 'What does all will to truth signify?' (*GM*, p. 297)

The unfolding of this conclusion will form a 'great spectacle of a hundred acts that will occupy Europe for the next two centuries' (ibid.).

Nietzsche knows that proclaiming the death of God will not put an end to the theistic worldview: there persists the 'shadow of God' – belief in a rational, orderly and moral universe – that remains to be overcome (*JW*, p. 151: para. 108). Unlike some post-Christian philosophers, Nietzsche does not believe that rationality and ethics can survive the demise of belief in God. His is a total scepticism in which both subject (the knower) and object (the known) are fictitious.

Nietzsche sets up Socrates as his antithesis, the arch-enemy of the Dionysan rapture. In *The Birth of Tragedy*, Socrates is presented as the embodiment of moralistic, analytical criticism; he is 'theoretical man', the 'dry-as-dust' scholar, the parasitic critic; founder of the mode of rationality that came to fruition in the Enlightenment; therefore the turning point and vortex of history. Socrates is the 'archetype of the theoretical optimist who, in his faith in the explicability of the nature of things, attributes the power of a panacea to knowledge and science and sees error as the embodiment of evil' (*BT*, pp. 71ff, 89). Nietzsche wishes to claim Kant and Schopenhauer as deconstructors of this tradition because they showed the limits of optimistic rationalism (pp. 87, 95). They picked up the thread of pre-Socratic philosophy that Socrates had severed (*HH*, pp. 123f: I. 261). Socrates remains Nietzsche's *bête noire*. *Twilight of the Idols* begins with a sustained attack on him: as well as his philosophical sins he was ugly and low-born – 'Socrates was rabble' – and was more than half in love with death, like the Christians (*TI*, pp. 29–34).

Nietzsche's metaphysical position, ethically and existentially, was one of 'azure solitude'. He stands upon the pinnacle, the mountain peak of existential intensity, regarding his fellow humans with disdain. Human community he viewed with revulsion. The more deserving of compassion and pity his fellow mortals were, the more Nietzsche was repelled. Christianity, for example, was distasteful to him as 'the revolt of the bungled and botched' (*WP*, I, p. 149: para. 179). Stern regards his persistent and systematic devaluation and denigration of all forms of human association as the most significant limitation of Neitzsche's thought (Stern 1979, pp. 127f). Barth sees his pathological individualism as the culmination of a strand in Enlightenment culture: 'The new thing in Nietzsche was the fact that the development of humanity without the fellow-man, which secretly had been the humanity of the Olympian Goethe and other classical figures as well as the more mediocre, reached in him a much more advanced, explosive, dangerous, and yet also vulnerable stage' (Barth, *CD*, III: 2, p. 240; see also pp. 231–242).

Nietzsche on Projection

Although Nietzsche lacks a theory of the mechanism of projection, such as that of Freud or Jung, he clearly operates with a general notion of projection. This conception is totalistic. As we have already seen, it is not that Nietzsche holds to a fundamentally rationalistic worldview, as does Freud, and sees religion as a chronic departure from this. For Nietzsche there is no unprojected world. Our entire universe is projected without remainder. The world is what we have made it. If it appears beautiful, it is because we have constructed it beautifully. If it seems rational to us, it is because we have made it rationally. If it impresses us as moral, it is because we have made it so.

In his early essay 'On Truth and Falsity in their Ultramoral Sense', Nietzsche already insists that all perception takes place by the creation of metaphors, though we make the mistake of taking them for the things in themselves. We inveterately and necessarily fashion the world after our image. When we discover some attribute of 'reality' – beauty, truth or goodness – it is like first hiding an object behind a bush, then triumphantly finding it there. Man can only live in security by forgetting that he is essentially an 'artistically creating subject'. Only what we add to the world (time, space, number, etc.) can be known to us, and these we produce out of ourselves as the spider spins from its own entrails. This metaphor-making propensity is expressed in myth and art as well as science and is at the root of our dreams. The boundary between reality and fantasy is blurred and fragile (*TF*, pp. 183–8).

In *Human, All too Human*, Nietzsche writes:

> Because we have for millennia made moral, aesthetic, religious demands on the world, looked upon it with blind desire, passion or fear, and abandoned ourselves to the bad habits of illogical thinking, this world has gradually *become* so marvellously variegated, frightful, meaningful, soulful, it has acquired colour – but we have been the colourists: it is the human intellect that has made appearance appear and transported its erroneous basic conceptions into things. (*HH*, p. 20: I. 16)

This is a recurring theme in Nietzsche. In *Twilight of the Idols* he reverts to it: 'Man believes that the world itself is filled with beauty – he *forgets* that is is he who has created it. He alone has bestowed beauty upon the world . . . Nothing is beautiful, only man' (*TI*, p. 78). And in the late fragments that comprise *The Will to Power*, we find Nietzsche asserting that all the beauty and sublimity with which we invest real and imagined things is truly the property and product of man; he has lavished these gifts on things to the impoverishment of himself (*WP*, p. 113).

It is in *The Will to Power* also that Nietzsche develops the notion of compensatory projection. Our idea of an unchanging, stable objective reality is the creation of our fear of change and decay. It is suffering that inspires these figments, the desire that such a world should exist, a revenge on the actual world that makes us suffer. Life weariness, not life, has created the metaphysical world (*WP*, passim; see also Schacht, pp. 163–5).

Applying this to religion and specifically Christianity, Nietzsche holds that all the gods of all the faiths are created to meet human needs. Religion came about when humans could not contain their overpowering, ecstatic feelings and attributed them to an external, transcendent source (*WP*, I, p. 113). The Greeks invented their gods to cope with the horrors of life (*BT*, p. 23). This was a nobler way of creating figments of the divine if create them we must, than that of the Christians, for the Greek gods gave divine legitimation to human vitality, the animal side of our nature, while the Christians, struggling with repressed desires, projected guilt, wretchedness and punishment – 'self-crucifixion' – on to the Christian pantheon (*GM*, p. 227). In Christianity, the negation of the natural self with its desires is reflected in a wrathful and oppressive God. On the other hand, the projection of noble ideals and perfections on to God is a prelude, a preparation, for the ultimate self-fulfilment of humanity and, in this respect, as Nietzsche sometimes admits, religion performs a useful role (*JW*, p. 234: para. 300). Nevertheless, it remains the case that God is a lie of man.

Nietzsche's Attack on Christianity

Nietzsche's chosen vocation was to destroy Christianity and the values that it stands for and to substitute an antithetical creed, based on the glorification of the life-force, the elemental power behind the cosmos and at the root of our existence that carries all before it, leaving no room for pity or compassion. His aim was nothing less than 'the transvaluation of all values'. But Nietzsche sought in vain to harden his heart against the sufferings of the world and to close up the springs of compassion. In 1889, moved by pity and indignation for a horse that was being abused by its driver in the street below his rooms in Turin, Nietzsche went down and threw his arms around the suffering animal. It was this act of solidarity with a fellow-suffering creature that precipitated his final descent into insanity.

Nevertheless, it is impossible to exaggerate Nietzsche's hostility to Christianity and the Christian Church. No rhetoric in this respect can outdo Nietzsche's own in which he styles himself 'The Antichrist' and 'Dionysus against the Crucified'. Nietzsche believed that he had gone further than the great anti-Christian polemicists of the Enlightenment. In 1884 he wrote to Overbeck: 'Since Voltaire, there has been no such attack on Christianity – and truth to tell, not even Voltaire had an inkling that Christianity could be attacked in *this* way' (Stern, p. 20).

However, it is essential to signal before we embark on an exposition of Nietzsche's critique of Christianity, that there is one very significant exception to his hostility: Nietzsche exempts the historical person of Jesus of Nazareth from his strictures. He makes a fundamental distinction between the human Jesus and the dogmas, pastoral methods and power-structures of the institutional Church. To this we shall shortly return.

Nietzsche is famous – or notorious – for his utterance 'God is dead'. *The Joyful Wisdom/ The Gay Science* tells of the madman who lit a lantern to look for God. The churches are the 'tombs and monuments of God' (JW, pp. 167ff: para. 125). *Thus Spake Zarathustra* begins with Zarathustra going down from the mountain with the knowledge that God is dead, amazed to discover that wise men did not yet know this. Part 2.2 expands on this assumption: God is a merely a supposition – an intolerable one. For if there were gods, who could bear not to be a god? And if there were a Creator, what would be left for us to create? 'Once you said "God" when you gazed upon distant seas; but now I have taught you to say "Superman" ' (Z, pp. 109ff). As Stern comments, Nietzsche's announcement is certainly meant to be performative (Stern. p. 143).

Nietzsche's greatest indictment against Christianity is that it is hostile to life, to beauty and to desire. Christianity's point of view, according to *The Birth of Tragedy*, is exclusively moral: it leaves no scope for the aesthetic. It is marked by '*hostility to life*, a furious, vindictive distaste for life itself' (*BT*, p. 8). In his essay on the philosophy of history, Nietzsche described Christianity as 'a religion which of all the hours of a man's life holds the last to be the most important, which prophesies an end to all life on earth and condemns all who live to live in the fifth act of a tragedy' (*UM*, pp. 101f). The dominantly moral Christian worldview, centred, according to Nietzsche, on guilt and punishment, comprises 'a hangman's metaphysics' (*TI*, p. 53).

In his later writings, Nietzsche singled out for criticism the traditional Christian hostility to eros, the Christian teachings on original sin, the demand for sexual abstinence, the Virgin Birth and the Immaculate Conception – so anticipating modern revisions of the Christian stance on these matters from broadly feminist theologians. As an expression of 'ressentiment against life', Christianity has made sexuality impure and polluted the origins of individual human life in sexual intercourse (*TI*, p. 110). In *The Antichrist* Nietzsche asks, 'Is it *allowable* to be a Christian as long as the origin of man is Christianized, that is to say, *dirtied*, with the concept of the *immaculata conceptio*?' (*A-X*, pp. 175f). In his final outburst *Ecce Homo*, Nietzsche proclaims that Christianity negates all aesthetic values, that it embodies a denial of the will to life, that it is the enemy of all vitality, and that the notion of 'God' is antithetical to life (*EH*, pp. 79, 121, 131f, 134). The final fragments contain the assertion that, while 'God on the cross' represents a curse on life, Dionysus contains the promise of life (*WP*, II, p. 421: para. 1052).

Christianity is the antithesis of the will to power, a denial and refusal of that *Macht* that is the source of all becoming. It glories in human weakness and has consistently taken the side of everything frail and vulnerable. The natural instincts that make for survival and success have been denigrated by Christianity. It is the 'religion of pity' (*A-X*, pp. 117f). In Christianity 'the bungled and botched', imperfect specimens of humanity, come into their own. Jesus and St Paul made the mistake of taking 'paltry people' seriously (*WP*, I, pp. 149, 171: paras 179, 205). The giving of infinite value to every human soul constitutes the 'raising of every sort of egoism to infinity' (A-X, p. 155).

Christianity preys on weak minds and wills making them dependent. It tracks down with the true hunter's instinct those who can be reduced to despair (D, p. 38: para. 64). It abases in order to uplift, burying man in the mud in order to shine a light on him (HH, p. 66: I. 114). Its methods of convicting of sin in order to offer divine forgiveness are a divine torture – it excels in tormenting the soul (D, p. 46: para. 77). Such notions as the Last Judgement and immortality are 'instruments of torture... forms of systematic cruelty' (A-X, p. 150). The diatribe against the priesthood in Zarathustra 2.4 speaks of those who know no other way of loving their God than by nailing people to a cross (Z, p. 115). Though, as is generally accepted, Nietzsche had not read Marx, he dubs Christianity a narcotic that induces passivity and obedience (JW, p. 181: para. 147). Christianity has declared even doubt to be sin: what it wants from the faithful is blindness, intoxication 'and an eternal song over the waves in which reason has drowned!' (D, p. 52: para. 89).

In its affirmation of weakness and dependence, the Christian faith has effected a 'revaluation of all the values of antiquity'. 'God on the cross' was – properly – foolishness to the Greeks (BGE, p. 57: para. 46). Christianity robbed Europe of the harvest of the culture of the ancient world (A-X, p. 183). But Nietzsche's revolutionary message would reverse this reversal.

Altogether, the Christian God is unworthy of deity. 'What sets us apart,' Nietzsche writes in The Antichrist, 'is not that we recognise no God... but that we find that which has been reverenced as God not "godlike" but pitiable, absurd, harmful, not merely an error but a crime against life... We deny God as God.' 'If this God of the Christians were proved to us to exist,' Nietzsche concludes, 'we should know even less how to believe in him.' In Christian faith the idea of God has reached an all-time low (A-X, pp. 128, 162f). The slogan 'God is dead', Nietzsche interprets elsewhere as meaning 'that the belief in the Christian God has become unworthy of belief' (JW, p. 275: para. 343).

What most offends Nietzsche is the crude anthropomorphism of traditional Christian teaching. Supernatural intervention is ludicrous and atonement by the blood of Christ 'gruesome' (*HH*, p. 66: I. 113). God as 'father', 'judge', 'rewarder' is implausible and offensive to the genuine religious sensitivities (*BGE*, p. 62: para. 53). It is our 'taste' that is offended by Christianity (*JW*, p. 173: para. 132).

For Nietzsche, the Christian religion is inseparable from its Jewish milieu and bears the unmistakable marks of Judaism. The phenomenon of Jesus Christ was only possible 'in a Jewish landscape', overhung by the gloomy thunderclouds of an angry Jehovah, among which Jesus could appear as a gleam of sunshine, a miracle of love. Christianity is altogether too oriental: it pictures an Eastern potentate who is swayed by feelings of *amour propre* and revenge (*JW*, pp. 173, 176: paras 132, 137; cf. *A-X*, pp. 134f: paras 24ff). On the other hand, Nietzsche has a deep respect for the Old Testament (at least compared with the New), finding in it great men, an heroic landscape, strong hearts, uncorrupted simplicity and a *Volk* (*GM*, p. 281). 'One stands in reverence and trembling before these remnants of what man once was' (*BGE*, p. 61: para. 52).

But Nietzsche feels nothing but revulsion for the New Testament – a collection of legends, literary remains of the apostles, and apocalyptic ravings not much better than Salvation Army penny tracts (*GM*, p. 281). The New Testament reeks of the stifling atmosphere of sickly devotion (*BGE*, p. 62: para. 52). It is driven by 'bad instincts' and lacks freedom, benevolence, open-heartedness and honesty. The early Christians have a bad smell and their book is unclean – to be handled with gloved fingers. Pontius Pilate is the only New Testament figure worthy of respect – because he challenged the crudity and bigotry of Christian claims with his question, 'What is truth?' (*A-X*, pp. 161f: para. 46). Nietzsche has what many Christians would regard as the audacity to discuss the IQ of Jesus of Nazareth, comparing him unfavourably with the superior intellect of Socrates who possessed 'that *wisdom full of roguishness* which constitutes the finest state of the human soul' (*HH*, p. 332: II. 2. 86).

For Christianity has always been, in Nietzsche's eyes, unscholarly and anti-intellectual. He had long since decided that, given the current state of knowledge, one could no longer be associated with it 'without incurably dirtying one's intellectual conscience and prostituting it before oneself and others' (*HH*, p. 61: I. 110). As an erstwhile professor of philology, Nietzsche was contemptuous of the way that Christian scholars interpreted their texts with an 'impudent arbitrariness' that provoked both rage and hilarity (*D*, p. 49: para. 84). The posthumously published fragments contain the indictment that Christianity 'is opposed to every form of intellectual movement, to all philosophy: it takes up the cudgels for idiots, and utters a curse upon all intellect' (*WP*, I, p. 130: para. 154).

Nietzsche is in no doubt about who to blame for the decadent character of Christianity: not Jesus of Nazareth but the apostle Paul – a tormented, pitiable and unpleasant individual. Paul was really the first Christian, the maker of Christianity and possessed a mind 'as superstitious as it was cunning'. Without him the world would hardly have heard of a small Jewish sect whose master was put to death on a cross (*D*, pp. 39f: para. 68). Paul, the 'dysevangelist', was the antithesis of Jesus: the one brought glad tidings, the other the logic of self-hatred (*A-X*, p. 154: para. 42). Paul corrupted Christianity into a bloody mystery religion (*WP*, I, pp. 136f: para. 167). In the opinion of some, Paul became more important than Socrates for Nietzsche as the revaluator of the virtues of antiquity, the prophet of *decadence* (Salaquarda in O'Flaherty, Sellner and Helm (eds.), p. 116).

For, in Nietzsche's judgement, the historical Jesus is not responsible for the religion that bears his name. As early as his essay on the philosophy of history, Nietzsche argues that the history of Christianity proves nothing about its founder: 'for if it did it would be evidence against him: between him and that historical success there lies a very dark and earthly stratum of passion, error, thirst for power and honour, of the continuing strength of the *imperium romanum*' (*UM*, p. 113, cf. p. 166). By the time of *The Antichrist*, Nietzsche is pointing out that the construction of the Church out of the antithesis of Christianity is a world-historical irony. In reality there has been only one Christian and he died on the cross. Jesus was interested in the truths of the heart alone. The kingdom of God was 'a condition of the heart'. The 'ecclesiastical crudities' of anthropormorphic dogma and eschatology were alien to him. He denied any chasm between God and humanity and therefore taught no doctrine of atonement. Jesus lived out the unity of God and man and this constituted his glad tidings. He lived and died to teach us how to live (*A-X*, pp. 146–54: paras 34–41). 'What did Christ deny?' Nietzsche asks in a late fragment; 'Everything which today is called Christian' (*WP*, I, p. 132: para. 158).

Assessment and Response

Frederick Copleston has aptly commented on Nietzsche that his increasingly shrill attack on Christianity was accompanied by an increasing inability to do justice to his foe (Copleston, p. 193). It is tempting to claim that Nietzsche directed his attack at Christianity's weakest points where, in its popular expressions, it is marked by superstition, lack of scholarship, bizarre interpretations, intemperate religious exercises, bigotry and the indulgence of all sorts of moral and personal hang-ups. But Nietzsche's onslaught is in fact directed not merely at the most inviting targets of Christian religiosity, but also at the substance and heart of traditional Christian belief.

It would also be possible to repay Nietzsche in his own coin for his genetic explanations of Christian faith. Just as he asserts that to identify the irrational sources of belief in primitive thinking is to discredit all religion without more ado, we could reply *ad hominem* that Nietzsche's hostility to Christianity, and above all to fervent devotion, can be traced back to the oppressive pietistic hothouse religion of his childhood home dominated by devout females. But if we are loath to accept his reductionist account of faith we cannot allow ourselves to fall into the same genetic fallacy. Nietzsche makes some substantial points about Christianity which require an answer in their own right.

Furthermore, it would be tempting to follow Pannenberg, in his discussion of modern forms of atheism, in attributing Nietzsche's entire anti-Christian platform to a misconceived emphasis on the will – with the clear implication that a better ontology would have avoided these excesses. Pannenberg maintains that Nietzsche's atheism is grounded in a view of the primacy of the human will which alone can attribute value to reality – even to God. Pannenberg believes that the tendency of nineteenth-century German Protestant theology played into the hands of the Nietzschian type of atheism. A. Ritschl (1822–89) – not to be confused with Nietzsche's mentor in philology F. Ritschl – and W. Herrmann (1846–1922), following Kant, made God a postulate of the practical reason and the deity of Christ a value judgement. Here, comments Pannenberg, 'the valuation of the human will was declared to be the native soil of the Christian faith.' Nietzsche's programme of the transvaluation of all values 'attained its maximum destructive power in relation to this theology'. For Ritschl, suggests Pannenberg, religion supports the human striving against nature; in Nietzsche this becomes a striving against God. The existentialist theologians of modern Protestant theology – M. Kahler, the early Barth, and Bultmann – with their emphasis on the 'decision of faith', are colluding with Nietzsche's assertion of the metaphysical primacy of the will. In denying the possibility of objectifying God in a natural knowledge of deity prior to the actualisation of faith in decision, the early Barth and Bultmann are giving unwitting succour to the typically modern form of atheism, the postulating of sheer, empty transcendence by a naked act of the human will à la Nietzsche (Pannenberg, 1971, pp. 193–9).

Once again, however, we have to insist that this sort of genealogical reduction of Nietzsche's critique of Christianity, valid though it is within its limits, is no substitute for a constructive response to the substantive criticisms that Nietzsche makes of the Christian tradition. Here we have to begin, I believe, with a frank admission that Christianity has often merited Nietzsche's condemnation. It has been hospitable to sadistic and masochistic tendencies on the part of its members and particularly its leaders. It has tormented consciences, indulged in guilt-mongering, and suppressed aspirations to freedom. It has consistently negated our natural, physical life, abolished beauty and denied eros. Anyone who has worked on the theological analysis of eros, as I have (Avis, 1989), is well aware that Nietzsche's diatribes are not too strong and that much of the Christian tradition deserves his strictures. The assumption that religion in general and the Christian religion in particular have been an unmitigated good for humanity has no place in Christian apologetics.

On the other hand, however, it has become apparent that the Christian tradition has within it the resources to correct and overcome these destructive tendencies and to develop a more wholesome theology that affirms life, beauty and desire as the gifts of God in creation – gifts that come to fulfilment when consecrated to that love of God that generates, enfolds and transcends them. Feminist theologies, theologies of embodiment and process theologies are correcting the distorted emphasis on divine transcendence which underlies many of the abuses that sickened and alienated Nietzsche. We have to say that we cannot now own the Christianity derided by Nietzsche. It is not the living faith of many Christians today. The Christian faith, as T. S. Eliot suggested, is constantly evolving into a faith capable of being believed. It has the creative capacity to respond to the insights and aspirations of humanity in every generation. Much Christianity in the West has long since digested Nietzsche's and others' criticisms and moved on. Christianity should respond to its arch-critic in modern times by deep heart-searching, profound repentance and setting out in search of a more excellent way. If, as I believe we must insist, the critique of Christianity is part of the essence of Christianity, to respond in this way is to make a thoroughly appropriate Christian response.

5

...eutic of Suspicion:
...mund Freud

... of Sinai, counting kine
...es, a patriarchal line
...rded mania on the sky?
...choliasts would not let it die?
(...ONQUEST, p. 103; 'Theology')

...ction between a hermeneutic of sus-
...ic of restoration has become indis-
...ke the latter first: a hermeneutic of
...by faith; it is fiduciary; it believes in
...proceeds by constructing a phenom-
...d is intended to lead to an apprehen-
...method of most modern theology
...cher onwards, has been acutely con-
...of hermeneutics, is a hermeneutic
...b the method employed by Jung in
...inted to the restorative, healing and
...ne symbols that emerge in dreams
...unconscious (as we shall see in detail

...ispicion – or, as Ricoeur calls it, of
...the other hand, is inspired by scepti-
...r to explain. It proceeds by exposing
...l aims to issue in enlightenment. It is
...er, antipathetic to religious belief, but
...l phase in the search for faith. Ricoeur
claims that it is the only viable way to belief in the modern
world: 'Today we can no longer hear and read the signs of the
approach of the Wholly Other except through the merciless
exercise of reductive hermeneutics.' Ricoeur concludes: 'Thus
the idols must die – so that symbols may live' (p. 531).
Freud is Ricoeur's prime exponent of the hermeneutic of
demystification or suspicion, though Feuerbach, Marx,

Nietzsche and Adorno belong to the same abrasive tradition of thought.

Biographical Background

Freud once referred to himself as 'a godless Jew' (Freud and Pfister, p. 63). Ernest Jones, Freud's official biographer, claimed that Freud went through life from beginning to end as a natural atheist. However, both in relation to Judaism and to Christianity, the picture is considerably more nuanced than both of those comments suggest.

Though he claimed to be totally irreligious and debunked the faith of his fathers, Freud never repudiated his Jewish identity and continued to identify with the Jewish people (see Gay; Clark, ch. 1; Scharfenberg, pp. 42–8; Meissner, pp. 24–56). All his life he was unwilling to accept royalties from translations of his work into Hebrew or Yiddish. He was acutely sensitive to any charge of anti-Semitism. The first circle of psychoanalysts was dominantly Jewish and Freud made few friends among Gentiles. His father came from a Hasidic background and elements of Jewish mysticism surface from time to time in Freud's work, though there is no evidence of acquaintance with the Talmud. Freud's mind was deeply affected by the liberal Jewish Philippson Bible with its vivid illustrations. He devoured these 'Old Testament' stories until he graduated to Shakespeare at the age of eight! His father sat light to the tradition; his mother's adherence was rather nominal. There was no synagogue in Freiburg, where Freud spent his earliest years. Freud married a devout Jew, Martha Bernays, and his refusal to allow Jewish observances in their household was a sore point between them, though often handled humorously on both sides. Freud's Jewishness should neither be made the explanation of his theories nor overlooked as irrelevant.

Freud identified with Joseph, the interpreter of dreams, and with Moses who led the chosen people to a new and better land at great personal sacrifice. Freud published his article on Michelangelo's statue of Moses anonymously in 1914 – it held a good deal of personal investment for him. For three weeks he had stood daily in front of the statue in Rome. Freud interprets the statue as depicting Moses, not about to smash the tablets, but struggling to contain and overcome his feelings – to sublimate them – so that he may continue to devote himself to the destiny of leadership to which he has been called. Moses then comes to stand for Freud's principle of cultural progress through the sublimation of instinctual drives. In his later work *Moses and Monotheism*, Freud distinguished between the biblical Moses, whom he portrayed as a primitive Midianite, worshipper of the fire-demon Yahweh, and the historical and historically significant Moses who was an Egyptian, representing the monotheistic religion of Aton, and who adopted the wretched Hebrew slaves who subsequently murdered him.

In the view of Peter Gay (pp. 31, 41), if Freud had been a religious believer he could not have developed psycho-analysis; he needed to be an atheist in order to scrutinise the psyche with such mordant suspicion. Freud once (1918) asked the Protestant pastor – his friend for thirty years – Oskar Pfister: 'Why was it that none of the pious ever discovered psychoanalysis? Why did it have to wait for a completely godless Jew?' (Freud and Pfister, p. 63). Pfister replied that it needed genius not just piety; that Freud was not a Jew (i.e. in faith rather than race), and certainly not godless, for all who dwell in love, as St John says, dwell in God – and psychoanalysis is a 'cure through love', as Freud once insisted to Jung. 'A better Christian there never was,' was Pfister's verdict. What was Freud's real relation to Christianity?

Freud was profoundly influenced by his Roman Catholic nursemaid, Resi Wittek, repressing the memory of her until the turn of the century. For protracted periods she had sole care of Sigmund and may well have been his wet-nurse. She instilled in the impressionable mind of this two or three year old Christian beliefs about God, judgement and hell. It is quite probable that she covertly baptised him. We know that she took him into all the (Roman Catholic) churches and when he came home he stood on a chair and pretended to preach. It seems probable that Freud's nanny was 'framed' by his mother to stifle her evidence of the mother's adultery with her stepson. There is a tradition that the nanny went to prison. It was at this point that the Freud family left Freiburg for Vienna. The separation from his nanny was traumatic for Freud and seems to have been the cause of his travel phobia.

The motif of the 'two mothers' is salient in Freud's discussions of Oedipus, Moses and Leonardo.

It has been plausibly suggested by Vitz in his comprehensive survey of Christian elements in Freud's life and thought, that Freud's longing to be reunited to his nanny/mother underlay his romantic feelings for the city of Rome, especially at Easter, his love of churches, and his profound emotional response to Christian art, and that his anger at what felt like betrayal by her and her religious world informs his deep fascination and identification with literary themes concerned with the demonic and occult, pacts with the devil, rebellion against God – notably in Goethe's *Faust* and Milton's *Paradise Lost*. Vitz comments that 'Freud's earliest, most basic experience of religion was connected to his earliest emotional attachment: it was traumatic; it was Catholic; and . . . it was the source of great ambivalence' (Vitz, p. 22).

It is easy to detect a defence mechanism operating in Freud's insistence that his childhood was non-religious. He equated religion with the childhood of the human race and of the individual, the world of illusion where the pleasure principle reigns. Scharfenberg speculates that in Freud's unconscious thinking the Catholic type of piety, connected with femininity, suffered a more rigorous repression than the Jewish Hasidic type, with its paternal associations: hence the dominance of the father complex in Freud's psychology (Scharfenberg, p. 110). Freud was deeply disappointed by his father, whom he regarded as morally weak and sexually perverse (there are dark hints of sexual abuse by the father among Freud's siblings). There were more reasons for Freud to feel hatred and resentment for his father, Jacob, than rivalry for the possession of his mother. In Oedipal terms, this suggests that Freud's identification with his father was thwarted. Deeply wounded by his nanny/mother but unable to make the transition to identification with the father – it is no wonder that Freud was left with a legacy of irresolvable psychological tensions which he attempted to work through in his theories. This applies no less to his theories of religion. Freud's experience in therapy with believing Jews or Christians was absolutely minimal. What then, was the source of Freud's knowledge of religion? What special knowledge enabled Freud to set himself up as an authority on the psychology of religion? As Vitz suggests, Freud was still working through the powerful emotions centred on his nanny and the world of Roman Catholic religiosity that she represented. Vitz goes so far as to suggest that 'the weight of psychological evidence now makes atheism a more probable symptom of neurosis than theism' (p. 221).

The philosophical influences on Freud are also ambiguous. He read Feuerbach's *The Essence of Christianity* while still at school and its theory of the projection of human wishes and ideals on to super-human divine figures underlies Freud's argument in *The Future of an Illusion*. It is significant that the core of Freud's theory of religion long predates his analytical work. He admitted himself – though only in private – that 'the views expressed in my book form no part of analytic theory. They are my personal views, which coincide with those of many non-analysts and pre-analysts, but there are certainly many excellent analysts who do not share them' (Freud and Pfister, p. 117). On the other hand, however, he was greatly impressed as a student with the Thomistic philosopher and Gestalt psychologist Franz Brentano (1838–1917) and attended assiduously his lecture courses, in which a theistic worldview was eloquently defended. The ambivalence persists.

Freud's engagement with the Christian faith was most explicit in his protracted correspondence with Oskar Pfister (1873–1956) – pastor, psychoanalyst, educationalist and prolific author. Freud regarded Pfister with genuine affection and respect, addressing him on one occasion as 'Dear Man of God', and expressed his satisfaction that 'a holy man like you has not allowed himself to be scared of such a heretical relationship' (Freud and Pfister, pp. 29, 83). Pfister was a welcome guest in the Freud household where, as Anna Freud recalled, he was like a visitor from another planet, with his clerical garb and ministerial bearing (p. 11). Pfister in turn praised the Freud menage as a haven of warmth, kindness and generosity (pp. 145ff).

At the beginning of their correspondence (1909) Freud explained to Pfister that psychoanalysis in itself was neither religious nor anti-religious, but an impartial tool which both priest and layman can use in the service of the sufferer. He confessed that, 'as a wicked pagan', alienated from the whole system of religious ideas, it had never occurred to him that psychoanalysis might be useful in pastoral work (p. 17). Twenty years' later, Freud returned to this thought, struck by the absurdity of his ever saying to a patient, 'I, Professor Sigmund Freud, forgive thee thy sins' (p. 125).

Pfister gently but firmly stuck to his liberal Protestant guns. He was unintimidated by Freud and was his match in scholarly productivity ('Your productivity is beginning to put mine to shame,' wrote Freud in 1924, 'and I have not been in the least lazy in my time': Freud and Pfister, p. 96). There was not much chance of either of them capitulating – Freud turning up for baptism or Pfister renouncing his pulpit (p. 121). He felt that Freud had performed a service to Christianity by making it look to its credentials: 'A powerful-minded opponent of religion is certainly of more service to it than a thousand useless supporters' (p. 110). Pfister described Freud's alternative to faith as the outlook of the eighteenth-century Enlightenment 'in proud modern guise' (p. 121f). Freud was indeed a step-child of the Enlightenment; Gay calls him 'the last of the philosophers' (p. 41). He could readily quote such luminaries of the Enlightenment as Voltaire, Diderot and Lessing and insisted that there was no court of appeal higher than reason. As a student in Vienna, however, Freud had reserved his greatest admiration for Feuerbach ('Among all philosophers, I worship and admire this man the most') – a far more radical and destructive critic of Christianity than the eighteenth-century deists (p. 53).

Pfister attributed Freud's hostility to religion to the fact that he grew up in contact with its 'pathological' manifestations, but gave him credit for being 'better and deeper' than his unbelief (Freud and Pfister, pp. 121f). Pfister did not believe that Freud's method necessarily carried reductionist consequences. Tracing the emergence of moral principles to childhood experiences does not invalidate them. 'Just as real love does not disappear when it is made clear that the first love-object was the mother,' Pfister argued, 'so does the ego-ideal not collapse when it is revealed that it originated with the parents' house. The parents may be right, and their moral demands may be the correct expression of a valid order of things' (p. 136).

Freud disclaimed any intention of setting up a rival worldview to Christianity or Judaism. He was dismissive of metaphysics: 'I believe that metaphysics will just have to be judged a "nuisance", a misuse of thinking' (Scharfenberg, p. 38). However, in his later work, Freud did turn to questions of worldview and to broader cultural perspectives, combining these with crude historical speculations, such as the theory of the primal horde. It is ironical that, as has so often been pointed out, psychoanalysis came to have all the appearance of a surrogate religion, with Freud himself as its first and greatest prophet and reigning high priest, its validated priesthood (the analysts), its dogma and discipline for maintaining doctrinal orthodoxy. As Gay says, science was Freud's faith (Gay, pp. 18f). Not that Freud was a rigorous positivist – he worked by intuition and flashes of insight, rather than by controlled observation and statistical analysis (Scharfenberg, pp. 38ff). He professed to Pfister in 1910 that the life of the imagination was all in all to him: 'I cannot face with comfort the idea of life without work; work and the free play of the imagination are for me the same thing, I take no pleasure in anything else.' Pfister chose to quote these words in his letter of condolence to Freud's widow nearly thirty years later (Freud and Pfister, pp. 35, 146).

The Theological Reception of Freud

Scharfenberg (p. 24) has observed that the theologians' picture of Freud 'exhibits astonishing contrasts, tensions and discrepancies. It shows with humiliating clarity the historically conditioned nature of theological knowledge.' Scharfenberg himself (p. 1) is one who agrees with Pfister that Freud's challenge has performed a better service to Christianity than a thousand useless supporters, but many interpreters would not agree. Neo-orthodoxy was particularly hostile.

Karl Barth dismissed any suggestion that theology could learn anything from Freud, depicting his theories as 'the gruesome morass of the psychology of the unconscious'. It offended Barth that in Freud's psychology the springs of human motivation and conduct were reduced 'to the very specifically sexual' (Scharfenberg, p. 12). It is interesting to compare this revulsion from explicit sexuality with the well-known and less admirable aspects of Barth's personal history and with his interpretation of the virgin conception of Jesus where he maintains that God's redemptive purpose in the incarnation had to by-pass the sexual relationship in order to be accomplished since eros is incompatible with agape and therefore cannot be the vehicle of divine grace (Barth *CD*, I/2. pp. 190ff; cf. Avis 1989, p. 112).

Emil Brunner detected in Freud's affirmation of the human person as a sexual being the makings of a pagan, erotic religion vaunting itself against divine revelation and redemption that countered all human pretensions (Scharfenberg, p. 12). Reinhold Niebuhr, similarly, giving his Gifford Lectures on the eve of the Second World War, identified Freud with the sinister irrational drives then manifestly threatening Christian civilisation. Freud's theories belonged to the 'romantic-materialist protest against rationalistic interpretations of human nature and history'. 'In Freudianism the dark labyrinths of man's unconscious impulses are illumined in such a way that he loses confidence in the pretensions of rational man and the disciplines of culture and civilisation.' Thus Freud's 'simple hedonism' can lead only to pessimism, despair and anarchy (Niebuhr, pp. 36, 54f). Neither Brunner nor Niebhur do justice to Freud's insistence on the dominance of the reality principle over against the pleasure principle, exemplified in his own life of arduous and unrelenting devotion to work, moral imperatives and civilised and cultured values.

However, twenty years later Niebuhr had arrived at a remarkably more positive assessment of Freud. In an essay 'Human Creativity and Self-Concern in Freud's Thought' (in Nelson) Niebuhr hailed Freud as 'one of the great scientific innovators of our era', commenting that 'the therapeutic efficacy' of his discoveries had been amply proved, bringing 'thrilling advances in the art of healing' (p. 259). Niebuhr saw Freud as an ally in theological realism because he had counteracted the facile optimism of the Enlightenment with regard to the perfectibility of human nature by insisting on the inevitability of 'egotistic corruptions of creativity'. Freud had provided the first scientific realist account of human behaviour (p. 260) and had discredited the Kantian and Hegelian god-like pretensions of human reason (p. 264). Niebuhr pondered the paradox of the therapeutic efficacy and political irrelevance of Freud's thought (p. 266). He concluded that the biblical doctrine of original sin was superior to Freud's analysis of the human condition because it placed the fault in human history, not in human nature, in the corruption of human freedom rather than in innate resistance to that freedom (pp. 275f).

By this time there were a number of Christian theologians who readily drew on Freud's insights. Pfister was perhaps the first – accepting Freud's therapeutic technique while resisting his worldview. Eduard Thurneysen, Barth's collaborator, regarded psychoanalysis as a 'helping science' for pastoral care (Scharfenberg, p. 14). In the later 1940s the Anglican clergyman R. S. Lee wrote his pioneering work on *Freud and Christianity* in which he claimed that religion must learn to come to terms with the scientifically established findings of psychoanalysis (pp. 18f) and used Freud's insights to shed a good deal of light on Christian symbols and myths. According to Lee, Freud raises the question for Christian theology: is Christianity the expression of an integrated and healthy psyche, based on the reality principle and our knowledge of the world as it really is, or is it merely the product of unreconstructed unconscious fantasies, driven by wish-fulfilment? (p. 87). Lee accepts that wish-fulfilment plays a large part in shaping our ideas of God. Psychoanalysis can help us to recognise this fact and so to discriminate between the relative worth of various motives and beliefs. It can help to free Christians from 'the thralldom of their unconscious motivation', to supersede infantile stages of development and to show what maturity in religious faith means. If, however, Christianity refuses the enlightenment that psychoanalysis brings and insists on clinging to neurotic manifestations of the unconscious in infantile dependence and blatant wish-fulfilment, it will deserve to perish (pp. 136, 192f, 197).

The theologian who is most hospitable to Freud's theories – though not uncritically so – is Paul Tillich. Tillich saw that neo-orthodox attacks on Freud were misplaced: psychoanalysis merely studies the dynamics of human encounter with the sacred; it can never impinge directly on divine revelation. 'It is not the task of theology', insisted Tillich in the first volume of his *Systematic Theology*, 'to protect the truth of revelation by attacking Freudian doctrines of libido, repression, and sublimation on religious grounds' – or for that matter, by defending the alternative Jungian doctrine as more conducive to revelation (Tillich 1953, 1, p. 145). Moreover, Freud's analysis of libido is justified in so far as it reveals that 'libidinous elements are present in the highest spiritual experiences'. This has always been known in the monastic tradition and agrees with Christianity's realistic evaluation of the human existential predicament. (Tillich parts company with Freud when he insists that creative eros must be capable of including sex; Freud's puritanical attitude to sex excluded this (pp. 61f).) Tillich's theology accommodated the theory of projection which, as he pointed out, is as old as philosophical thought itself. Every projection is not only a projection *of* something, but also a projection *upon* something. Our images of the sacred, such as the father-image, are projected on to the screen of 'the unconditional'. There is indeed, as Freud showed, a connection between the Oedipus complex and the historical development of religion and morality. The nature of childhood experience, in a patriarchal culture, is such that God is inevitably pictured as Father. When this is taken literally, it leads to neurotic infantile dependence. The father-image has become demonic by being idolatrously identified with the unconditional. Critical enlightenment, including psychotherapy, can help to correct this distortion (Tillich, 1964 (1959), pp. 140ff; Perry, ch. 4).

A major contemporary apologist for Christianity, Hans Küng (b. 1928), adopts an ambivalent attitude to Freud's thought: admiring of Freud as a man and open to his critical insights and their relevance to theology and the Church, while discounting his specific theories of the origins of religion (Küng 1990 (1979)). Küng agrees that Freud's theory of the primal horde, the murder of the patriarch and the perpetuation of the crime together with its simultaneous atonement in a sacramental (totemistic) meal seems 'unworthy of a scholar', and points out that 'nowhere did Freud find less support than for his views on ethnology and history of religion' (pp. 40, 66). Like Meissner, Küng dismisses Freud's procrustean evolutionary framework: all serious scholars question the imposition of a doctrinaire systematic evolutionism on the history of religion. 'Religions have developed in a wholly and entirely unsystematic pluri-formity' (p. 67).

Küng focuses on Freud's critique of religion as 'illusion' (cf. Freud, *The Future of an Illusion*, 1927). In designating religion an illusion, Freud did not mean that religion is a deliberate lie in the moral sense, nor that it is an error of perception and interpretation of data in the epistemological sense; nor is it necessarily illusory in the sense of being unrealistic or opposed to reality (Judaism at least adhered to the 'reality principle'). Illusion is driven by wish fulfilment. Religion arises out of the oldest, strongest and most urgent wishes of humanity. Illusion is motivated by longings emerging from the fundamental sensual and instinctual level of life. Freud accepts that this verdict on the aetiology of religion cannot decide the question of its truth content. Küng quotes Freud: 'To assess the truth-value of religious doctrine does not lie within the scope of the present enquiry. It is enough for us that we have recognised them as being, in their psychological nature, illusions' (Küng, pp. 46f).

Of course Freud, as an atheist and a materialist, certainly did believe that the doctrines of religions were false, but as Küng points out, Freud's atheism went back to his school days; it was not grounded in his psychoanalysis. Freud's ideological atheism was not a necessary conclusion of his methodological atheism. The validity of the theory of projection as a psychological mechanism does not prove that there is nothing to project on to. Freud adopted at an early stage the projection theory of Feuerbach together with its reductionist connotations. But as Küng concedes, 'from the psychological standpoint belief in God always exhibits the structure and content of a projection . . . The mere fact of projection, therefore, does not decide the existence or non-existence of the object to which it refers' (pp. 77f). Küng's stance – accepting a good deal of Freud's fundamental approach, including the reality of projection, but not his specific conclusions about religion – suggests the lines on which the problem of reductionism will be resolved in the final section of this chapter.

Freud's Interpretation of Religion

In alliance with anthropological theories derived mainly from Darwin and Roberson Smith, Freud employed the concept of projection to construct an explanatory theory of religion. In Freud there is an analogy – indeed more than an analogy, an isomorphism – between the source of religion in the individual and its origins in the race (ontogenetic and phylogenetic). In both, a basic feeling of helplessness in the face of the environment is the spur to attempts to influence it by projection (*PFL*, 12, pp. 202, 205): in the case of the infant, by manipulating the parents to obtain its wants, in the case of the race, by anthropomorphising nature, thus taming its mystery. As Freud wrote in *The Future of an Illusion* (1927):

> Impersonal forces and destinies cannot be approached; they remain eternally remote. But ... if everywhere in nature there are Beings around us of a kind that we know in our own society, then we can breathe freely, can feel at home in the uncanny and can deal by psychical means with our senseless anxiety. (p. 196)

From these animistic beginnings, an inventory of religious ideas is built up, born from humanity's need to make its helplessness tolerable and incorporating the memories of the helplessness of the childhood of the individual and of the infancy of the race (p. 198). 'The infant's helplessness and the longing for the father aroused by it ... is permanently sustained by fear of the superior power of Fate' (*Civilisation and its Discontents*, 1930, p. 260).

As the child craves the protection of his human father, so the race longs for the protective care of an all-powerful cosmic Father. 'Thus the benevolent rule of a divine providence allays our fear of the dangers of life; the establishment of a moral world-order ensures the fulfilment of the demands of justice ... and the prolongation of earthly existence in a future life provides the local and temporal framework in which these wish-fulfilments shall take place' (*PFL*, 12, p. 212). Freud claims that this is the verdict of psychoanalysis: it reveals that a person's god 'is formed in the likeness of his father, that his personal relation to God depends on his relation to his father in the flesh and oscillates and changes along with that relation, and that at bottom God is nothing other than an exalted father' (*Totem and Taboo*, 1913, p. 209).

It is not entirely clear how the origin of religion in 'the humanisation of nature' by projection, which Freud describes in *The Future of an Illusion* is to be reconciled with the theory of the murder of the patriarch of the primal horde by his rebellious sons that Freud advanced in *Totem and Taboo* and reiterated in *Civilisation and its Discontents* and *Moses and Monotheism*. In the first account, religion is a response to weakness and fear, in the second, it is the expression of guilt. The former is universal in its potential application; the latter only really lends itself to Judaism and Christianity where it is reactivated by the (supposed) murder of Moses. What both theories have in common, however, is that they are both, in Freud's view, interpretations of religion as an illusion derived from human wishes (*PFL*, 12, p. 212f).

What must be granted to Freud is that a great deal of Christianity is blatantly a form of infantile wish-fulfilment in which God is required to be both daddy and mummy. Believers weave a cocoon of illusory comfort and assurance around themselves. Their self-induced conviction, confirmed by warm feelings and trivial 'providential' coincidences, is unfalsifiable since everything that happens is grist to their mill. If all goes smoothly, God must have been busy behind the scenes, preparing the way of his servants. If trouble strikes, God is trying their faith and is still in control. Everything is still 'all right'. As Freud comments, 'the whole thing is so patently infantile, so foreign to reality' (*PFL*, 12, pp. 261, cf., 273).

This transparently infantile and illusory faith is wide open to Freud's strictures. But more sophisticated and 'adult' versions of the Christian faith, that have been through the fires of human conflict or personal tragedy, and reflect the doctrine of a suffering God working through God's people to overcome injustice, prejudice and pain, are not so easily dismissed.

The connection Freud postulates between the two aspects of his theory of religion, the universal cosmic projection of human attributes, as described by Feuerbach, and the particular, historical crime that gave rise to religious myth and ritual, is found in the suggestion that 'the primal father was the original image of God, the model on which later generations have shaped the figure of God' (*PFL*, 12, p. 225). Freud maintains therefore that 'the store of religious ideas include not only wish-fulfilments but important historical recollections' (p. 226). It is this second aspect of religion that particularly, in Freud's view, gives it its 'neurotic' character.

Just as the child represses the memory of his infant traumas, especially those centring on the Oedipus complex, so too the race has repressed the feelings of guilt and remorse generated by that primal crime. And just as failure to assimilate or come to terms with the legacy of repressed emotions can result in an obsessional neurosis, so too the religious life with its obsessive rituals, especially the communal meal, is the neurotic expression of the unexorcised repressed feelings of the race. Religion is thus 'the universal obsessional neurosis of humanity' and 'like the obsessional neurosis of children, it arose out of the Oedipus complex, out of the relation to the father' (*PFL*, 12, p. 226). Now just as the neurosis of the individual can be helped by analysis, as repressed irrational fears are brought out into the conscious light of day and subjected to rational, objective assessment, so too the neurosis of the race, religion, is bound to fade away in the light of the growth and dissemination of scientific knowledge. Religion, like neurosis, serves a purpose; it expresses and contains genuine emotions derived from actual experiences, but, argues Freud in *The Future of an Illusion*, 'the time has probably come, as it does in an analytic treatment, for replacing the effects of repression by the results of the rational operation of the intellect' (pp. 227f). For Freud, as for Marx, there is no such thing as enlightened religion, for enlightenment spells the end of religion.

Evaluation of Freud on Religion

It is easy enough to discredit Freud's theory of religion by showing that his reconstruction of the historical origins of Mosaic monotheism (involving the hypothesis that Moses was an Egyptian and that he was murdered by the Hebrews) is untenable and that his scenario of the prototypical murder of the patriarch of the primal horde is, at the very least, unprovable. On Freud's premises, historical objections would be important, even perhaps decisive, for he was clear that there could be no return of the repressed unless a traumatic event had actually occurred and been repressed. But a purely genetic response to Freud, though it would be paying him back in his own coin, would at the same time fall into the same (genetic) fallacy that Freud himself succumbed to. It would be comparable to debunking artistic culture because (on Freud's principles) it is the product of sublimated sexual energy. That reductionist approach does not answer the question of what culture – or religion – have become and what value they now have, or are capable of attaining.

In his exhaustive study *Psychoanalysis and Religious Experience*, W. W. Meissner SJ has exposed the untenability of Freud's reconstruction of the historical origins of the Hebrew religion, based on his use of Wellhausen, in the light of recent research; and this is a useful thing to have done. More to the point, however, is Meissner's argument that Freud's account is purely genetic and reductionist. On *The Future of an Illusion*, Meissner comments: 'The weight of the argument supports no conclusion further than that religion often serves as a matrix within which the displaced fantasies of infantile residues find expression' (p. 60). Such a conclusion does not refute Christianity: it is merely grist to the mill of Christian prophets and reformers in attacking the perennial religious tendency to commit idolatry by projecting our thoughts which are not God's thoughts, and our ways which are not God's ways, and making God in our own image. The criticism no more discredits religion as such than the perception that the displaced fantasies of infantile residues operate in the world of politics (cf. Lasswell) discredits political life. Rather, as Meissner points out, 'The critical question is whether the dynamism of religious belief has an inherent capacity to supersede its own archaisms.' And, in Meissner's view, 'An investigation of the instinctual substrate of religion can hope to provide no more than a partial answer' (p. 68). A more careful discrimination of these so-called 'infantile residues' is called for, and here the psychotherapist Harry Guntrip has a useful contribution to make.

Guntrip has effectively drawn the string of Freud's critique of religion as infantile regression, wish fulfilment and unre-constructed dependence on the father, by distinguishing between immature or neurotic dependence and mature rational dependence (or as we might say, interdependence), pointing out that the latter is a permanent feature of human nature. Guntrip concedes that religion, dealing as it does with the emotional needs of human beings as persons, will always be liable to import infantile dependence into its motive springs. But he sees nothing immature or neurotic about our hope that our life as persons arises out of, and depends upon, a profoundly personal principle grounded in the structure of reality. Such a belief is not self-validating and it is the task of philosophers and theologians to show whether it can be justified, but, Guntrip insists, 'he would be a bold, foolish man who should insist that it is in itself a neurotic wish.' He further suggests that 'it would be an easier task to prove, on psycho-analytic grounds, that a sustained attitude of solitary defiance of an indifferent, impersonal ultimate reality' – and here he has Bertrand Russell in mind – is neurotic. This is, of course, a defence of religion in principle, and certainly not of every manifestation of it. But Guntrip insists that critique based on psycho-analytical principles, like that of Freud, is misdirected when used to exclude religion as such from its sombre worldview. Psychotherapy is only properly concerned with helping individuals to deal with immature dependence of an infantile character (pp. 383f).

It is clearly integral to Meissner's case – and to mine throughout this book – not to deny the role of illusion, in the sense of the projection of meaning on to reality, in religion. As we have seen earlier, it is through putting out projections, that can be withdrawn again when the time is ripe, that we explore our world. Projection (or as Meissner prefers, illusion) is a mode of transition to reality – provided of course that our projections can be corrected: uncorrected they become illusion or, psychologically speaking, neurosis. Meissner usefully reminds us (pp. 164–84) of D. W. Winni-cott's notion of 'transitional objects' such as a comforter or teddy, by means of which a child makes the difficult and sometimes painful adjustment from identifying with the mother and the mother's breast to relating to external reality. Without a capacity to utilise transitional objects in order to generate transitional forms of experience, the child's attempts to gain a foothold in reality will be frustrated. This sort of projection (or illusion, as Meissner will have it) is the vehicle by which we gain access to reality. Religion is a realm of transitional experience, between human subjectivity and transcendent reality. Religious symbols are transitional objects, comprising both subjective and objective aspects. The real, objective, material world – water, bread, wine, lights, flowers, places, and so on – is experienced, penetrated, and reshaped by our human subjectivity (Meissner, p. 181). The product of this conjunction is the realm of the sacred, through which we know God, not as he is in himself, but as he has willed to reveal himself, clothed in the garments of creaturely reality.

6
God or the Unconscious?
C. G. Jung

I know a night of stars within me;
Through eyes of dream I have perceived
Blest apparitions who would win me
Home to what innocence believed.
(SIEGFRIED SASSOON, p. 300; 'Human
Bondage')

If Freud's approach is the epitome of a hermeneutic of suspicion, leading to theological reductionism, Jung's method,
by contrast, appears to have all the marks of a hermeneutic
of affirmation, leading to theological restoration. Freud's
assumptions are materialist and positivist. His explanations
of psychological events trace them back to physiological
functions. The body is ultimate, the spirit epiphenomenal.
Jung's assumptions – though, as we shall see, they claimed to
be just as rigorously empiricist as Freud's – are informed
from beginning to end by a profound regard for spiritual
values. His explanations of psychological events trace them
back to the numinous, the transcendent, the sacred – to
religion and 'God'. Spirit is primary, the body is its vehicle.
Jung went as far as to claim to one correspondent: 'The main
interest of my work is not concerned with the treatment of
neuroses but rather with the approach to the numinous.' This
brought the real therapy and numinous experience released
one from 'the curse of pathology' (Jung 1973, 1, p. 376). As
A. Storr points out, there is a contrast in their ultimate values.
While Freud found supreme value in the orgasmic release of
sex, Jung attributed ultimate value to the unifying experience
of religion (Storr, p. 19).

Thus, while Freud saw the unconscious as the repository
of hostile forces waiting for the opportunity to spring out and
ambush the unsuspecting individual in the form of conversion
hysterias (psychosomatic paralysis, for example) or phobias,

Jung, though equally wary of the irrational and untamed powers of the unconscious, saw it as the matrix of healing symbols that contain virtue with the potential to impart wholeness to the personality. These symbols emerge from the unconscious under psychological pressure. They mediate the ultimate psychic structures, the archetypes of the collective unconscious which themselves are completely inaccessible. As Jung used to insist, echoing the Bible, no man has ever seen an archetype. Archetypal images are like the stars in the heavens: coming from afar, ultimately inaccessible, numinous, yet shedding a light upon our life. It is interesting to pursue the stellar analogy a bit further.

Jung believed that the stars played an insignificant part in the mental life of primitive peoples, and attributed the projection of the constellations and the symbolic significance of the stars to the rise of reflective consciousness. He ventured the conclusion that we originally read our first physical and particularly psychological insights in the stars. They become symbols of revelation. 'What is farthest is actually nearest' because it corresponds to the structure of the unconscious (Jung 1973, 2, p. 564). All forms of human creativity draw on the unconscious – music, literature, art, scientific discovery. Van Gogh seems to have been an artist who was particularly receptive to the unconscious. His painting *The Starry Night* (1889), now in the New York Museum of Modern Art, makes the stars great looming presences like lanterns in the sky. They do not twinkle but glow, radiant orbs, in a sky that is alive with movement, swirling and eddying above the sleeping village and its little church with the elongated spire. This is clearly a parable of the unconscious – the 'night of stars within' – that stirs when we sleep. But it is also a parable of the role of the church which, with its spire acting like a lightning conductor, is in contact with the mysterious unfathomable forces around and above it. But do the sleeping villagers know this? Does the minister, who will open up his church in the morning, when all this vision will have passed away, know this?

Jung and Christianity

Jung always regarded Freud as a brilliant innovator and continued all his life to pay tribute to his pioneering genius in the exploration of the unconscious. For a few years Jung also regarded Freud as a father-figure while Freud looked on Jung as a son and heir. The traumatic break with Freud was ultimately a religious issue. Freud's attitude to religion in any form, Jung insisted, was a negative one. 'Religious belief to him was indeed an illusion ... He was unable to admit anything beyond the horizon of his scientific materialism.' Jung claimed to have tried, unsuccessfully, to show Freud the error of his ways (1973, 2, p. 295). At the end of his life, Jung's thoughts returned to the question of Freud's hostility to religion. Jung claimed to have seen for himself in the years of their collaboration that Freud was beset by anxiety, stemming from a fear of Yahweh which is always present in the unconscious in Judaeo-Christian culture, and is imprinted particularly deeply in the Jewish mentality (p. 575). This was not anti-Semitism coming out in Jung. He was well aware that he had had to wrestle with the same problem symbolised for him in dreams by the dark ecclesiastical figures who approached menacingly. But Jung resolved it differently and more constructively than Freud, by grappling with the shadow of the Old Testament God, notably in his *Answer to Job*, and finding the divine persona reconciled in the incarnation and the corresponding image in the psyche, that of the self. So here, remarkably, Freud and Jung had something fundamental in common.

It might seem, then, that Jung is an ally of Christianity, who can be deployed to bolster theology and compensate for the damage done to the credibility of the Christian faith by Freud's radically reductionist theories of religion. Such a conclusion would, however, be premature. Jung does indeed defend spiritual realities – but not the interpretation that traditional Christianity has placed upon them. Theology should certainly look to Jung for enlightenment – but it will find itself profoundly changed if it does so. If Christian theology wants to appeal to Jung's authority, it can only do so at the cost of finding itself somewhat relativised and treated on the same footing as, for example, comparative mythology,

Eastern religions, Gnosticism, medieval alchemy and Goethe's *Faust*. For Jung regards all these as cultural expressions of the eternal archetypes of the collective unconscious that figure in humanity's spiritual pilgrimage. Does that mean that Jung treats all these manifestations as of equal value or that he declined to identify himself with any of them?

In his early thought Jung is more outspoken about the relativisation of Christianity, writing for example in 1933: 'I positively do not believe that Christianity is the only and the highest manifestation of the truth. There is at least as much truth in Buddhism, and in other religions too' (1973, 1, p. 127). Soon afterwards he advised a pastor, who was beginning to doubt his vocation, that Christianity would be needed for a long time to come; the great majority of people should be content with it in its present form; but since dogma is symbolic, Christianity cannot be ultimate (pp. 191f). Twenty years later Jung warned Victor White that the end of the Christian aeon was approaching and, as Joachim of Fiore had foretold eight centuries before, the age of the Paraclete would dawn. 'We are actually living in the time of the splitting of the world and of the invalidation of Christ,' Jung wrote. 'Christ is still the valid symbol. Only God can "invalidate" him through the Paraclete' (1973, 2, pp. 137f). Jung's remarks here are cryptic and mysterious. The splitting of the world refers to the Iron Curtain between East and West which Jung saw as profoundly symbolic, and the Paraclete presumably to a rebirth of the Spirit, following the splitting or division of the world, bringing hope of a universal experience of God. However, it is worth nothing that Jung is still working with Christian symbols even though he seems to be proposing a transcending of the particularity of Jesus Christ. In the last year of his long life, Jung wrote to a pastor: 'Although I profess myself a Christian, I am at the same time convinced that the chaotic contemporary situation shows that present day Christianity is not the final truth' (p. 575). Generally speaking, Jung roundly assures his correspondents that he is a Christian and a Protestant to boot, though he continues to speak bitterly of the churches and theologians. It seems safe to say that Jung regarded the Christian faith as the highest – though not the absolute – form of the evolution of the religious consciousness.

The question that concerns us here, however, is whether, in interpreting Christian beliefs in terms of archetypal symbols, Jung is not eliminating the objective transcendent reference that is intrinsic to Christian truth claims and so effecting a radical reduction to purely subjective, immanent realities. The issue is whether Jung's approach, while satisfyingly 'spiritual' in its ethos, is not ultimately as subversive of Christian theology as Freud's. Is Jung also to be numbered among the reductionists?

Biographical Background

Jung's personal attitude to Christianity was ambivalent. His life was a walk with 'God', surrounded by a halo of numinosity. He regarded the reality of God as a 'given', almost as a tautology. 'What mankind has called "God" from time immemorial you experience every day, you only give him another, so-called "rational" name,' Jung wrote to a sceptical correspondent. 'Why do you ask about God at all?' he continued, 'God effervesces in you and sets you to the most wondrous speculations' (1973, 2, pp. 4f). Jung confessed to Erich Neumann that he was 'held in thrall, almost crushed' by the experience of God, and tried to defend himself as best he could (p. 33). God resided at the 'innermost self' of every human being and of all creatures, animate and inanimate, though 'infinitely diminished' (p. 120). Towards the end of his life he wrote to a Benedictine: 'I find that all my thoughts circle round God like the planets round the sun, and are as irresistibly attracted by him. I would feel it most heinous sin were I to offer any resistance to this compelling force' (p. 236). Again he wrote of the inescapability of God: 'God is an immediate experience of a very primordial nature, one of the most natural products of our mental life, as the birds sing, as the wind whistles, like the thunder of the surf' (p. 253). God, Jung writes in extreme old age, is the name we give to all overpowering emotions in the psyche; we encounter God mastering us, subduing our conscious will and taking over (p. 525).

Jung's reply, when asked in the celebrated interview with John Freeman in 1959 whether he believed in God, is famous: 'I don't need to believe, I know.' Though he afterwards pretended that he had been caught unawares by the question, the fact is that Jung had often spoken in these terms. In an interview with Frederic Sands for the *Daily Mail* in 1955 Jung spoke of his 'unshakeable conviction of the existence of God'. 'I do not take his existence on belief,' Jung affirmed, 'I know that he exists' (Brome, p. 255). Jung consistently tended to oppose understanding and belief, writing for example in 1948 to Victor White the Dominican theologian with whom he had endless and inconclusive conversations, in person and by letter, over many years: 'I can say my life-work is essentially an attempt to understand what others apparently can believe' (1973, 1, p. 502). Jung stated a few years later: 'People speak of *belief* when they have lost *knowledge*. Belief and disbelief in God are mere surrogates.' Primitive people do not believe, they know on the strength of inner experience (1973, 2, p. 5). Jung confessed bitterly: 'Since my earliest youth I have been made to feel how rich and how knowing the believers are and how disinclined even to listen to anything else ... I am not concerned with what is "believable" but simply with what is knowable.' He writes, not for believers, for they think that they already have all the answers, but solely for unbelievers (p. 197). Answering a questionnaire from a researcher in 1955, Jung replied to the question 'Do you believe in a personal God?' with the words: 'I don't *believe*, but I do know of a power of a very personal nature and an irresistible influence. I call it "God" ' (p. 274). Jung's longest statement on this question comes in a letter of 1959 when he was well into his eighties, and was in response to a letter arising out of the John Freeman interview. He knew of God-images in universal experience and in his own psychic life. 'It is the experience of my will over against another and very often stronger will, crossing my path often with seemingly disastrous results, putting strange ideas into my head and manoeuvring my fate ... outside my knowledge and my intention' (p. 522). Here Jung appears to equate God with the unconscious, and that is a problem that we shall take up shortly.

Compared, however, with his immediate experience, Jung came to regard institutional Christianity as a betrayal of the numinous. In his autobiography *Memories, Dreams, Reflections*, Jung, a son of the manse, claims to have seen through the religiosity of the vicarage and parish church at an early age. His confirmation merely set the seal on his disillusionment. Already experiencing, so he claimed, the reality of the numinous through dreams and fantasies, he was shattered by the ordinariness of church worship. The Christian ministry acquired morbid associations for him and Jesus Christ became a god of death not life, of bloody crucifixion, not joyful resurrection. Eight uncles were parsons: Jung always seemed to picture them officiating solemnly at funerals in their black frock coats and shiny black boots. Similarly, his dreams and fantasies were haunted by black hooded Jesuitical figures who approached menacingly. As a child he fell and hurt his head in a Roman Catholic Church and thereafter was assailed by fears of falling whenever he entered one (Brome, pp. 35ff). All churches had a disturbing effect on him: when once unexpectedly compelled to lecture to teachers from a church pulpit it gave him 'such a shock' that he avoided such locations thereafter (1973, 2, p. 128).

According to Jung, his father grappled with insoluble theological dilemmas and was eventually crushed by them. Jung took up for himself his father's quest, but sought the answers not in supposedly revealed theological propositions but in the revelations of his inner world. 'It was the tragedy of my youth,' Jung recalled in old age, 'to see my father cracking up before my eyes on the problem of his faith and dying an early death' (1973, 2, p. 257). Roaming at large through his father's library, Jung took up the vast Reformed dogmatics of Biedermann, but it seemed to him 'fancy drivel . . . a specimen of uncommon stupidity whose sole aim was to obscure truth' (Brome, p. 50). Jung retained a lifelong suspicion of theologians. They were scholastic, dry-as-dust dogmaticians who lacked a knowledge of the inner life of the soul. Jung once said to Archbishop William Temple: 'Send me an intelligent young theologian. I will lead him into the night of the soul so that at least one of them at last may know what he is actually dealing with'. His offer was not taken up. 'Naturally they knew it all already, and much better. That is why the light has gone out' (1973, 1, pp. 372f). Jung's pleasure was unfeigned when he found understanding and appreciation from a theologian in the person of Victor White OP – though Jung took it equally to heart the other way when White would not come round to his point of view on the nature of good and evil. Generally, Roman Catholic theologians were more open to his approach than Protestants – perhaps because they retained a grasp of mystery and of the role of sacred symbols. Jung deplored the impoverishment of symbolism in Protestant thought and worship (though he rightly made an exception of Paul Tillich) and remarked that Protestant theologians had not yet decided whether he was to be condemned as a heretic or deprecated as a mystic (p. 382). But Jung insisted that his work belonged to the ethos of Protestantism which drew its vitality from its encounter with the spirit of the age – of which psychology was now a part. If it fails in this task, it dries up. Already it is beginning to wither (1973, 2, p. 287; cf. p. 77). Jung's great objection to theologians is that they would not admit that their talk of God was inescapably anthropomorphic and that the ultimate mystery eluded them. They could not engage in dialogue, but could only preach six feet above contradiction. This attitude was what had alienated him from the church, Jung claimed (p. 114). Jung's *Answer to Job*, which his American publishers refused to take, in which he exposed the moral and psychological deficiencies of Yahweh, taking Job's part against his Maker, 'released an avalanche of prejudice, misunderstanding, and above all, atrocious stupidity' (1973, 2, p. 115).

As a boy, then, he had come to the conclusion that church was not the place for him, and he later rather pointedly commented that an individual's decision not to belong to a church does not necessarily denote an anti-Christian attitude. It may equally well indicate a quest for the kingdom of God in the heart where the Christian mystery is accomplished 'in its inward and higher meanings' (quoting St Augustine) (Jung 1983b, p. 32). The religion of Christendom, by contrast, may be largely an outward veneer. The evidence of history – and above all of the first half of the twentieth century – Jung suggests, is that the springs of the inner life of Western humanity remain unscathed by Christian influence – 'pagan and archaic'. A Christian may believe all the dogmas of Christianity and possess a complete inventory of its sacred symbols, but these may all remain external to his or her essential inner life (*SW*, p. 261).

Interpreters disagree on the true value of Jung's professed allegiance to the Christian faith. P. Homans remarks that writers like H. Schaer who baptise Jung's psychotherapy and place it at the service of the Christian cure of souls, and Victor White himself who went with Jung as far as he could without contradicting Catholic dogma, 'have not given sufficient attention to the massive evidence which supports Jung's life-long struggle to repudiate Christianity – to free himself from its oppressive claims upon his life. Nor do they see the great extent to which Jung, in his mature writings, found traditional Christianity utterly incomprehensible' (Homans in Moore and Meckel, eds, p. 23). It is true that Jung frequently departs from his purported phenomenological, objective approach to interject the comment that Christian dogma, taken literally, is unintelligible and repellant. Why then, as Storr correctly insists (Jung 1983a, p. 13), did Jung explicitly declare his allegiance to Christianity? The truth is that Jung took Christianity in an enlightened, 'higher' sense, interpreting its doctrines spiritually and symbolically, not historically and literally. We shall want to expand on this method and its implications shortly.

Jung – a Reductionist?

Jung's interest in religion is in the original numinous experience that has the force of revelation. This experience is shown by comparative studies to have a common symbolic structure, conforming to the archetypes of the collective unconscious. The creeds are propositional expressions of this symbolic experience of the numinous, and Christian doctrines have their symbolic equivalents in the archetypal themes of mythology and alchemy. Jung insists on the abiding validity of religion and regards it as a great therapeutic system, helping to maintain equilibrium in the psyche. The stages of therapy can be matched with the phases of Christian pastoral care (see Avis 1989, ch. 9). The human psyche, according to Jung, is 'by nature religious' (1983a, p. 12). Ideas of moral order and of God belong to 'the ineradicable substrate of the human soul' (1985, p. 64). The archetypal images are eternal: they have 'peopled the heavens of all races from time immemorial' (n.d., p. 112). Every religion is the spontaneous expression of 'a certain predominant psychological condition' (*CW*, 11, p. 97), and as the psychological condition varies from culture to culture and from one period of history to another, so its religious expression will vary. As we shall see, even the figure of Christ is not exempt from this principle of psychological relativity. Thus religion is absolutised but religions are relativised.

Jung's critical analysis of 'God' (the inverted commas are necessary at this stage), which came to a head with *Answer to Job* (German 1952; English 1954) incurred the wrath of theologians and pastors who took him to be attacking divine revelation, church dogma, holy Scripture, etc, and accused him of just about all the heresies in the book from gnosticism to atheism. Jung was acutely sensitive to these charges and his rebuttals display indignation and defensiveness in roughly equal proportions. He points out repeatedly that one must appreciate the fundamental difference between two distinct approaches to the question of God. One is the empirical, phemomenological, scientific approach, which Jung himself espouses. The other is the metaphysical, theological approach which he firmly eschews. He is merely the humble empiricist, describing what he sees. It is not God but the image of God in the psyche that is the subject of his analysis. He makes no attempt to pronounce on the metaphysical implications of his findings. This principle of demarcation is stated as early as *Symbols of Transformation*:

> The divine figure is in the first place a psychic image, a complex of archetypal ideas which faith equates with a metaphysical entity. Science has no competence to pass judgement on this equation: on the contrary, it must pursue its explanations without resorting to any such hypothesis ... Science can only establish the existence of psychic factors. (*CW*, 5, p. 61)

It would be a great mistake, Jung insisted, to criticise his conclusions as though they were expressions of his personal religious opinions. He is neither challenging Christian orthodoxy nor presupposing its truth. He is merely looking at the human side of religion, and as far as this phenomenological approach is concerned, all religions are on the same footing. 'The psychologist, if he takes up a scientific attitude, has to discard the claim of every creed to be the unique and eternal truth. He must keep his eye on the human side of the religious problem, since he is concerned with the original religious experience quite apart from what the creeds have made of it' (*CW*, 11, p. 9).

Let me illustrate Jung's defence of his method from his letters. Replying to the superintendent of a sanatorium as early as 1933, Jung protested that he found it 'exceedingly odd' that he should 'amiably take me for an atheist'. Recalling that Kant too (and we shall return to the authority of Kant for Jung) had been taken for an atheist by some of his contemporaries, Jung explained, 'When I treat of the concept of God I am referring exclusively to its psychology and not to its hypostasis.' Though he has theological views of his own, 'they cannot be known to you since I have never expressed them. When, therefore, you state in your estimable letter that you know exactly what kind of God I believe in, I can only marvel at your powers of imagination' (1973, 1, pp. 123ff).

Jung was also accused of atheism in a hostile book by Pastor M. Frischnecht published in 1945. Jung retorted: 'Your opinion that I am an atheist is pretty bold, to say the least . . . What do you know, may I be permitted to ask, about my religious convictions?' Jung deplores his critic's assumption that he identifies the psychic God-image with God and protests that physicians from time immemorial have brought healing through anamnesis of the archetypes. They were doing this when 'parsons still wore leopard skins and danced to the drum' (1, pp. 359ff).

Early in his extended correspondence with Victor White OP, Jung was constrained to justify his approach. When he had described God as a complex, 'I meant to say: Whatever he is, he is *at least* a very tangible complex . . . I surely never intended to say: He is nothing else but a complex.' To White's accusation that he rejects divine transcendence, Jung replies: 'This is not quite correct. I merely omit it since I am unable to prove it . . . I am not a theologian and have nothing to say about the nature of God' (1973, 1, pp. 384ff). To another correspondent Jung insisted: 'Psychology as a natural science must reserve the right to treat all assertions that cannot be verified empirically as projections. This epistemological restriction says nothing either for or against the possibility of a transcendent Being. Projection is an unavoidable instrument of cognition' (1973, 2, p. 6).

To Fritz Buri Jung explained that he never made statements about a metaphysical God. 'I speak always and exclusively only of the anthropomorphic God-image' (1973, 2, p. 64). And replying to Dorothee Hoch, who had reviewed his *Job*, Jung emphasised the autonomy of psychic images. 'As a psychologist I have to speak of ideas professionally and if necessary criticise them when they behave objectionably. I don't imagine that by so doing I have affected God' (p. 66).

One of the most powerful attacks on Jung came from Martin Buber, following the publication of *Answer to Job*. Buber branded Jung as a gnostic. Jung was scathing about Buber's ignorance of psychology. Buber, asserted Jung, believes that a metaphysical assertion must be either true or untrue and does not understand that as a psychologist and psychiatrist he viewed all metaphysical beliefs purely phenomenologically. 'Why can't Buber get it into his head that I deal with psychic facts and not with metaphysical assertions?' Jung professes amazement that intelligent people could take his models and hypotheses as theological assertions about ultimate reality (1973, 2, pp. 367, 370f, 570ff). Buber seems unaware of the existence of the unconscious and of the autonomy of complexes, though they have shown themselves to be 'devastatingly real', says Jung. Anyone who remains sceptical should take a thoughtful tour of a lunatic asylum (*CW*, 18, pp. 663ff).

Victor White OP quotes a letter 'written to a theologian' (actually himself) in 1945 where Jung explains: 'I never allow myself to make statements about the divine entity, since this would be a transgression beyond the limit of science ... As a scientist I must give a wide berth to anything dogmatic or metaphysical, since it is not the scientist's task to preach the gospel' (White, p. 72; Jung 1973 1, p 384). How consistent was Jung in refraining from preaching? What were his views about the competence of metaphysics? How far does he reveal his own metaphysical commitments?

Jung and Metaphysics

Jung's apparently modest eschewal of metaphysical specu-
lation is actually somewhat disingenuous. He not only
believed that it was not for the empirical scientist to venture
beyond the data, he also believed that the nature of ultimate
reality was foreclosed to human minds. He not only ruled
out metaphysics for himself, but cast doubt on its value at
all. When he insists that 'what God is in himself remains a
question outside the competence of all psychology' (Jung
1985, p. 65), he also means that it is a question outside the
competence of theology and philosophy.

Jung's epistemology is unquestionably idealist. Mind or
spirit was ultimate and the structure of the human mind
contained the key to reality. In her treatment of Jung's philosophical outlook, M. Nagy argues that he approached idealist
monism: 'in his most far-reaching meditations, we are breath-
ing in an atmosphere in which the things of the mind are all in
all' (Nagy, p. 35). But Jung's reading of Kant had permanently
marked his thinking, making him a *critical* idealist, for whom
the intuitions of intellect were subject to the analysis of
experience. Moreover he had no time for Hegel's brand
of absolute idealism. Jung's idealism was mediated by the
Romantics, especially Schleiermacher. For a man as conscious
of the living influence of his ancestors as Jung, it is not
surprising that he continued to acknowledge the impact of
Schleiermacher – himself a distinctly post-Kantian thinker –
upon his family tradition. 'Schleiermacher really is one of my
spiritual ancestors,' he wrote, claiming that Schleiermacher
had baptised (rebaptised?) his grandfather as an adult convert
from Roman Catholicism to Protestantism. 'The vast, esoteric, and individual spirit of Schleiermacher was a part of
the intellectual atmosphere of my father's family . . . uncon-
sciously he was for me a *spiritus rector*' (1973, 2, p. 115).

It coheres with his affinity with the Romantics and Goethe,
his philosophical allegiance to the mid-nineteenth century
(especially Schopenhauer's emphasis on destiny as the out-
working of an ultimate Will), and his distaste for the analytical and linguistic turn of twentieth-century thought, that
Jung should have been sympathetic to the perennial *vitalistic*
tradition with its antecedents in the Renaissance and alchemy.

Jung combined his vitalism with a fully Aristotelian teleology which sees the immanent life-force working out its purpose, ultimately through the process of self-reflective individuation in humanity. The source of this immanent dynamic are the archetypes of the collective unconscious. For Jung they are the 'transcendent' instinctual source both of psychic energy or libido and of psychic structure or images. Nagy, who has brought out the vitalistic commitments of Jung's position, is justified – ironically, in view of Jung's repeated disclaimers – in concluding that Jung's theory of archetypes is incontestably metaphysical (Nagy, pp. 144, 265ff).

Jung's stance as an empiricist reflects the Kantian distinction between *phenomena* and *noumena*, stiffened with a strong dash of nineteenth-century positivism no better than Freud's. Jung's writings gave ample testimony to the fact that he accepted Kant's veto on knowledge of *noumena*. 'I consider it presumptuous to credit human knowledge with a faculty that demonstrably exceeds its limitations,' he replied to a critic as early as 1933 (1973, 1, p. 125). The metaphysical reality of God far exceeds the limits of the theory of knowledge, Jung insists to a pastor in 1935 (1973 1, p. 195). A metaphysical God, Jung maintains to Dorothee Hoch, is beyond the range of human understanding (1973, 2, p. 66). Epistemological criticism, Jung insists elsewhere, proves the impossibility of knowing God, but the psyche comes forward with the fact of the experience of God. This reveals God to be both a psychical phenomena and an archetype, but says nothing about a transcendent being correlative to either (Jung *CW*, 8, p. 625; 7, p. 110). In his eighties (1957), Jung roundly declares that 'everything men assert about God is twaddle, for no man can know God. Knowing means seeing a thing in such a way that all can know it, and for me it means absolutely nothing if I profess a knowledge which I alone possess. Such people are found in the lunatic asylum' (1973, 2, p. 377). Difficult as this may be to square with Jung's confessions in the Sands and Freeman interviews, it certainly reinforces his commitment to the Kantian metaphysical veto.

Jung is not always as reticent as he claims to be about his own theological views. He confides to Victor White, for example, in 1945, his personal belief that human vital energy or libido is to be identified with the divine spirit (*pneuma*)

(1973, 1, p. 384). Jung is also dismissive of the received tenet of theism that God is (by analogy at least) personal:

> The naive assumption that the creator of the world is a conscious being must be regarded as a disastrous preju-dice which later gave rise to the most incredible dislo-cations of logic ... Divine unconsciousness and lack of reflection ... enable us to form a conception of God which puts his actions beyond moral judgement and allows no conflict to arise between goodness and beastli-ness. (Jung 1984, p. 33n)

It would surely be stretching language unreasonably to take this statement as referring merely to the God-image and not to a God 'out there'. Having touched also on the vexed question of Jung's understanding of the nature of good and evil, it will be as well to say something more about this here.

On the question of evil, Jung moves, in the way that is by now familiar to us, from protestations that he is merely interpreting psychical phenomena to frankly metaphysical claims. Psychology cannot judge between good and evil. As Jung put it in *Job*, psychology does not know what good and evil are in themselves; it knows them only as judgements about relationships. The unconscious makes no difference between good and evil (1984, p. 53). The God of the Old Testament, Yahweh, has an unacknowledged shadow and acts unreasonably, unfairly and vindictively. Job challenges divine injustice and exposes the shadow. In the New Testament the incarnation represents God emerging from the state of being the 'victim of unreflected opposites'. This is precisely the answer to Job. But it could not happen without the figure of the devil becoming more distinct (in the Old Testament and explicitly in Job, Satan is a heavenly figure, residing in the presence of God, almost an aspect of the divine nature). The devil is Christ's shadow with which he is reunited in the cross and which he transcends in the resurrection (1973, 2, pp. 164f, 240). Because the opposites have to become rec-onciled and integrated in the divine nature (*coincidentia oppositorum*), it is impossible for a reflecting consciousness to believe that God is aptly described as the *Summum Bonum* (1984, p. 93).

Apart from the *Answer to Job*, the main source for Jung's

views on this question is his correspondence with Victor White OP, who maintained uncompromisingly the Catholic Thomistic doctrine that God is the *Summum Bonum* and evil is the mere absence of good (*privatio boni*) or non-being (Greek *me on*).

Jung insisted to White in 1949 that the matter of good and evil, so far as he was concerned with it, had nothing to do with metaphysics but was purely a psychological statement. His insistence on the reality of evil and his rejection of Roman Catholic dogma on this point did not make him a 'Neo-Manichean'. Nor did it make him a *psychological* dualist: 'I am deeply convinced of the unity of the self, as demonstrated by the mandala symbolism.' Paradoxically, however, Jung did detect dualism lurking in the shadows of Christian doctrine since the devil would not be redeemed nor eternal punishment ever come to an end. But Jung's concern, before, during and after the Second World War, was for the future of humanity which he believed could not be secured without taking the shadow – the dark, alien side of human nature – with all seriousness. As long as evil was defined as non-being, the absence of good, no one would take his own shadow seriously. 'The future of mankind very much depends upon the recognition of the shadow. Evil is – psychologically speaking – terribly real.' It is a fatal mistake to diminish the power and reality of evil metaphysically, for this no longer corresponds to psychical reality – though the psychical realities of good and evil should not be projected on to a transcendent being (1973, 1, pp. 540f). At the height of the Cold War, Jung wrote to White that he wanted to shake the unconscious of his contemporaries, to teach them to acknowledge their shadow – just as Job had revealed Yahweh's shadow – in order to avert nuclear catastrophe (1973, 2, p. 239).

Jung insisted to White that good and evil are revealed empirically in psychological analysis to be two sides of the same coin, inseparable aspects of a logical judgement, like black and white, darkness and light, right and left: 'On the practical level, the *privatio boni* doctrine is morally dangerous because it belittles and irrealizes evil and thereby weakens the good, because it deprives it of its necessary opposite . . . If evil is an illusion, good is necessarily illusory too . . . The moral opposites are an epistemological necessity' (1973, 2,

p. 61; cf. pp. 52f). In a long letter Jung told White: 'From the psychological standpoint the experience of God the creator is the perception of an overpowering impulse issuing from the sphere of the unconscious. We don't know whether this influence or compulsion deserves to be called good or evil' (p. 134).

Now when a patient undergoing therapy emerges from the sway of the unconscious, he is confronted by his shadow and is compelled to decide for the good, since the first step on the path of individuation is discrimination between oneself and one's shadow (1973, 2, p. 135). Jung spoke feelingly about the baneful influence of his own shadow and kept a bust of Voltaire in his patients' waiting room so that his grinning, cynical, mocking visage (not unlike the depiction of the archetypal figure of the trickster) might counteract his patients' naive, optimistic and distorted expectations of the benevolent, genial miracle-working analyst behind the next door (pp. 267f).

However, Jung finds it impossible to keep his assertions about the nature of good and evil on the phenomenological plane. Claiming that the Catholic doctrines of God as the *Summum Bonum* and evil as *privatio boni* were non-logical, symbolic expressions (though distorted) of psychological realities, Jung went on to assert that God was neither good nor evil but transcendental like the self and not subject to human logic. Though this statement can be taken at the purely psychological level, Jung certainly believed in the objective existence of the self – and this raises the likelihood that he posited the objective existence of a metaphysical God beyond good and evil (1973, 2, pp. 52f). Jung also talks in blatantly metaphysical language when he writes to Victor White in a pronounced Kantian vein: 'If you assume, as I do, that good is a moral judgement and not substantial in itself, then evil is its opposite and just as non-substantial as the first. If however you assume that good is being then evil can be nothing else than non-being' (p. 72). Clearly Jung did go on to make metaphysical statements. Perhaps the truth is that in doing so he allowed himself to be guided by the unconscious and believed that, because he was being faithful to the unconscious he was avoiding metaphysics.

God and the Self

According to Jung, analysis of the psychical contents of dreams and other analytical material reveals an apparent identity, an isomorphism, of God and the self. Analysis cannot distinguish between the God-image and the self-image. They are not empirically or phenomenologically distinct. Jung goes so far as to say that worship is directed towards the psychic God-image as 'psychic energy or libido creates the God-image by making use of archetypal patterns' and so humanity 'worships the psychic force within him as something divine' (*CW*, 5, p. 86). Images of quaternity, of the squared circle, the mandala, that emerge in dreams (as well as in myths and religious symbolism) are revelations of 'the God within' (*CW*, 11, p. 58). These all fill out an original archetype of *wholeness*. For Christians, and generally in Western culture, the archetype of wholeness generates the Christological symbol of selfhood and this Christ-image has redemptive power. God, Christ and self are thus correlated in the psyche (*CW*, 5, p. 368). For this reason the doctrine of the incarnation and the process of individuation (the making of selfhood) are analogous: both are manifestations of the archetype of wholeness within human nature (*CW*, 11, p. 157; 1984, passim). For example, Jung writes in *Aion*:

> The spontaneous symbols of the self, or of wholeness, cannot in practice be distinguished from a God-image ... there is an ever-present archetype of wholeness which may easily disappear from the purview of consciousness or may never be perceived at all until a consciousness illuminated by conversion recognises in it the figure of Christ. As a result of this 'anamnesis' the original state of oneness with the God-image is restored. (*CW*, 9, ii, p. 40)

Jung is clear, however, that it is only in the West, in Christian cultures, that Christ functions as the God-image and symbol of the self. In the East his place is taken by Buddha or Krishna. For anything that I postulate as a greater totality than myself can function as a symbol of the self. Nevertheless, for Christians the symbol of Christ is absolute. He 'occupies the centre of the Christian mandala' (*CW*, 11, pp. 88ff, 152ff; 9, ii, p. 36).

The isomorphism of the images of self, God and Christ gave a further handle to Jung's critics who accused him of identifying God with the unconscious. Jung explicitly denied this identification. 'This is certainly not to say that what we call the unconscious is identical with God or is set up in his place. It is simply the medium from which religious experience seems to flow' (*CW*, 10, p. 565). As Forsyth rightly insists in his recent book on Freud and Jung, God and the self are not identified in Jung's thought, but at the level of experience they are indistinguishable (Forsyth, p. 113). Jung accused his critics – especially the theologians and pastors – of manufacturing a God out of words and then projecting that construct on to him. But he spoke from personal knowledge of these realities. 'I thank God every day', he wrote with some feeling, 'that I have been permitted to experience the reality of the *imago Dei* in me.' Without that experience he would have been a bitter enemy of Christianity and the Church. 'Thanks to this *actus gratiae* my life has meaning and my inner eye was opened to the beauty and grandeur of dogma' (1973, 1, p. 487).

It is interesting that Jung considers the question – and leaves it open – whether God is the image of the self, or the self is the image of God. Similarly he asks: 'Is the self a symbol of Christ, or is Christ a symbol of the self?' (*CW*, 11, p. 190; 9, ii, p. 68). Jung is emphatic that psychological investigation cannot resolve the problem either way.

> The parallel . . . between Christ and the self is not to be taken as anything more than a psychological one . . . There is no question of any intrusion into the sphere of metaphysics, i.e., of faith. The images of God and Christ which man's religious fantasy projects cannot avoid being anthropomorphic and are admitted to be so; hence they are capable of psychological elucidation like any other symbols. (*CW*, 9, ii, p. 67)

It is also important to note that Jung insists that the human figure in the centre of the Christian mandala 'is not a substitute but a symbol for the deity' (*CW*, 11, p. 96).

On the other hand, the psychical reality of the numinous

presence that we call God, does not in itself establish the objective, ontological reality of God. This is the converse of the question of reductionism in Jung. He deplores the use of his theories to prove the existence of God. They prove only the existence of the archetypal God-image, and as far as Jung is concerned, that is the most that can be claimed on psychological grounds (*CW*, 11, pp. 58f).

How does the Christ-image function therapeutically in the life of the believer, according to Jung? The key is the Christ figure at the centre of the Christian mandala. It is striking that this was anticipated by Dante. In his final vision of the Holy Trinity, Dante saw three mutually reflecting circles, and in the centre of the second a human form (Dante, p. 499). We recognise this pattern as a mandala, a symbol of wholeness and integration. The human figure at its centre is a symbol of the union of humanity and deity, which is the ultimate aim of the individuation process (Jung *CW*, 11, p. 96). For Christians, the figure at the centre of the mandala is Christ (*CW*, 9, ii, p. 26; *SW*, p. 267). The Christ-image, then, stands for the ideal of the self, its wholeness, integration and perfection. By conforming ourselves to it, through contemplation and ethical practice, we find our true self and discover the true meaning of our life. 'Through the Christ symbol, man can get to know the real meaning of his suffering: he is on the way to realising his wholeness' (*CW*, 11, p. 157).

It is quite arguable that Jung has here shed light on the psychological dynamics involved in the New Testament's teaching about the unity of the believer with Christ in his death and resurrection by reckoning oneself alive to God and setting one's mind on the things of Christ that are above, for example in Romans 6 and Colossians 3. A Gaelic prayer sums up what it means to be the subject of the process of the mutual drawing together and ultimate merging of the image of the self and the image of Christ: 'I find thee throned in my heart, my Lord Jesus. It is enough. I know that thou art throned in heaven. My heart and heaven are one' (Appleton, p. 57).

At this point, the theologically trained reader of Jung becomes uneasy (again!). Are we losing contact with the Christ of the gospels? Are we not getting the Jesus of history and the Christ of faith terribly confused? Jung's views about

Jesus and the Christ myth are more appropriately reserved for a sequel to this book, when we shall consider symbol and myth in some depth. For the present we may note that as far as Jung was concerned the historical figure of Jesus of Nazareth and the symbolic figure of the Christ are now abstractions. The historical and the ideal components of the construction 'Jesus as the Christ' cannot be separated out any longer. Jung does not doubt the historical reality of Jesus or the authenticity of many of the 'supernatural' deeds attributed to him. In him actuality and symbolic meaning became fused and can no longer be disentangled. 'I cannot prove the identity of an historical personage with a psychological archetype,' Jung writes to a pastor in 1955. 'That is why I stop after establishing the fact that in the Occident this archetype, or this 'God-image' is seen in Christ; in the Orient in the Buddha, or in the form of Tao . . .' (1973, 2, p. 267).

Does Jung Subvert Christian Theology?

We now need to ask, by way of summing up and conclusions, whether Jung's view of Christianity is compatible with traditional Christian truth claims. As we have seen, Jung believed that he had posed a radical challenge to Christian theology – has he actually subverted, invalidated, it?

The question is whether Jung has effected a gigantic exercise in reductionism, a conversion of deity into humanity, transcendence into immanence, the objective into the subjective. This would be a transmutation (to borrow Jung's favoured alchemical vocabulary) more plausible and attractive, and therefore more dangerous to theology, than Feuerbach's or Freud's head-on challenge. The possibility of such radical reductionism is suggested when Jung postulates that projections of God (and the demonic for that matter) might eventually be withdrawn into the psyche without remainder (CW, 11, p. 85). Pannenberg for one has interpreted Jung as turning 'the transcendence of God . . . into a psychic transcendence of the self over the ego,' and he has endorsed Keintzel's accusations of 'psychic inflation', of 'distending the ego' (Pannenberg, 1985, p. 264).

However, I am not convinced that Pannenberg and

Keintzel have understood Jung correctly. He is not advocating puffing up the ego by absorption of the unconscious, now emerging into consciousness, and he specifically warns against psychic inflation that can be produced by identifying with the archetypes (1983b, p. 101). He is speaking about a communion with the sacred that transcends our individuality. The archetypes belong to the collective unconscious: 'They represent the life and essence of a non-individual psyche' which can never be possessed by the individual personally. The collective unconscious is 'the precondition of each individual psyche, just as the sea is the carrier of the individual wave' (p. 5).

Even when he talks of withdrawing projections from the figure of Jesus to enrich the symbols of Godmanhood in the psyche, he does not imply that the figure of Jesus is dispensable. It is a misunderstanding, Jung complains in reply to Buber, that when a projection is withdrawn nothing more of the object remains. 'When I correct my mistaken opinion of a man I have not negated him and caused him to vanish; on the contrary, I see him more nearly as he is (*CW*, 18, p. 668). If Jung's own words are to be given credence, yet another suspicion of reductionism is here allayed.

In speaking of a realm of the sacred, of eternal numinous archetypes – Sassoon's 'night of stars within' us – Jung may be postulating no more and no less than the epistemology of Christian theology itself does. Theology acknowledges that we have no direct, unmediated, univocal knowledge of God and no direct, unmediated, unadulterated experience of God. Even divine revelation comes to us, as Barth rightly insisted, 'clothed in the garments of creaturely reality' – in and through the forms, structures and processes of the created world. Victor White argued that Jung's distinction between the God-image studied by psychology and God in himself 'should satisfy the most exacting and cautious theologian, for, on his account also, God infinitely transcends every image, concept or name that can be used of him' (White, p. 71).

What Jung has done is to help bring to light the forms, processes and structures of the unconscious life of humanity. Once we accept the conclusions of depth psychology as to the vital and determinative importance of the unconscious – which we can do without taking sides with one school of thought over against another – it would seem to follow that we should expect the grace of God and the word of God to be at work there also; perhaps we should say, there above all.

Jung believes, like Freud, that 'religious feelings are rooted in unconscious memories of certain tender emotions in early infancy.' But, for Jung, these are only the symbols with which the archetype of divinity clothes itself (CW, 5, p. 90). The fact that, according to Jung, these forms and structures appear as images of mother, father, anima, animus, old wise man, shadow, trickster, and so on, is perhaps no more remarkable or objectionable than the fact that for Christians the grace of God should take the form of bread and wine, a baby in a manger, a man on a cross, 'our Father in heaven', mother church, and so on. The Christian faith sees all these as instances of the graciousness, humility and condescension of the God who empties himself and takes the form of a servant. The way in which Jung's researches have illuminated the correlation between the symbols that originate from the unconscious and the tangible paraphernalia of the religious life is not the least of his contributions to the enlightenment of theology in the modern world.

Victor White OP as a Christian theologian with competence in analytical psychology, has argued on Jung's premises for the ontological priority of the archetype over the antitype:

> Behind the particularised physical mother's womb lies the archetypal womb of the Great Mother of all living; behind the physical father the archetypal Father, behind the child the *puer aeternus*; behind the particular manifestation of the procreative sexual libido lies the universal creative and recreative Spirit. The second of all these pairs appears now not as a phantasy substitute for the first, but rather does the first appear as a particular manifestation of the second. (White, pp. 56f)

The way is now open to us, White concludes, 'no longer to conceive of God as a substitute for the physical father, but rather the physical father as the infant's first substitute for God' (p. 57). Like Karl Barth, who stands the traditional doctrine of analogy on its head, White invokes the text (Eph 3: 14) which speaks of 'the Father from whom all fatherhood in heaven and in earth is named'.

Jung undoubtedly makes room for this approach. As his disciple and colleague M.-L. von Franz writes: 'Jung stressed that he definitely believed in the possibility of the metaphysical reality of religious contents, although there is no possibility of investigating such contents psychologically' (p. 52). Jung himself, while remaining extremely cautious about 'the further metaphysical significance that may possibly underlie archetypal statements', adds: 'There is nothing to stop their ultimate ramifications from penetrating to the very ground of the universe. We alone are the dumb ones if we fail to notice it.' We cannot pretend, Jung concludes, that the object of the archetypal images has been explained or disposed of merely by an investigation into the psychological aspects (*CW*, 11, p. 200).

The possibility emerges, therefore, of reversing the apparently reductionist consequences of Jung's approach in the interests of a theology that respects the ineffable mystery of God and allows this to condition its claim concerning divine revelation, while at the same time affirming the reality of the all-encompassing sacred realm. Some remarks of John Beer on Coleridge's *Aids to Reflection*, encourage us in this aspiration. Coleridge's approach, writes Beer,

> rests for its ultimate point on the supposition that the mirror in the mind does not simply reflect but opens out into another room, which you can see but never get into; that you cannot fully appreciate reflections on the waters of the mind unless you learn to look into the depths of the waters as well; and that the reflection in the world that best corresponds to the human psyche is that of the moon, which draws all its illumination from a hidden sun. (Beer, p. 242)

7
The Social Projection of the Sacred

The Frankfurt School

For the critical theorists of the Frankfurt School, who attempted to integrate Marx and Freud, sociology and psychoanalysis, religion is a projection of human subjectivity. For Horkheimer, 'religion is the record of the wishes, desires and accusations of countless generations' (1972, p. 129). For Adorno, the concept of revelation was a response to a transcendental anxiety generated by inner-worldly fears that have no answer (Siebert, 1983, p. 112). For Habermas, the ontological, metaphysical reality postulated by religion is a projection of practical, inter-personal communicative rationality, a gigantic inflation of the ideal of truly human discourse.

The critical theorists, who were almost without exception Jews (Habermas, the most important living exponent of the tradition of the Frankfurt School, is a Gentile), were motivated in their hostility to both Hegelian idealism and Christian theology by reverence for the second commandment. They regarded all talk of the unity of human and divine, of the embodiment of the Absolute, of Christology, as idolatrous. Fromm characterised all history as the history of idol-worship, from primitive totems to modern consumer or sexual fetishes. The individual alienated from his true self is necessarily an idolater: he projects and transfers vital inner powers on to an external object. The worship of an objectified part of the self is taken as worship of God. Projection on to the cosmos, in the concept of totality, is an alienated and idolatrous representation of one's own creative potential (pp. 54ff). In the Frankfurt School's critique of religion there is also the moral, social and existential protest against any invocation of totality in a totally administered society. In an alienated world, insists Adorno, the whole is the untrue; totality can only be radically evil. Theology, for the critical theorists Horkheimer and Adorno, is an expression of humanity's unappeasable longing for justice, a rationalisation of hope deferred, of the refusal of the human spirit to accept that the murderer should ultimately triumph over his innocent victim (Siebert 1985, pp. 115f, 155, 159; 1983, p. 109; Jay, 1984b).

If their Jewishness predisposed them to a theological iconoclasm that appealed to the second commandment, their materialism and atheism led the critical theorists to reduce all religion to the projection of human longing. As such, it perpetuated a state of dependence, unfreedom and thwarted fulfilment. Whereas Schleiermacher and Feuerbach saw a sense of dependence as the primary religious impulse, for Horkheimer 'religion is not based on dependence but on autonomy and freedom' (Siebert 1985, p. 134). Any objectification of the Absolute is not only theologically blasphemous, but morally undesirable. A transcendent Absolute offers an ultimate horizon for human hope and a critique of all human attainment. An embodied Absolute reduces the tension, trivialises hope and legitimises the status quo. For Horkheimer the transcendent, for Adorno utopia, place a limit on all totalitarian pretensions.

This is precisely the point at which the question of the objective reality of the transcendent becomes crucial. The critical theorists give no ground for hoping and believing that the Absolute exists outside of human consciousness. Horkheimer's courageous affirmation of the transcendent in his old age is ultimately an illusion to overcome illusion. As far as Adorno is concerned, only once in his entire dialectical philosophy and sociology (Siebert tells us; 1985, p. 369) did he break his self-imposed vow of obedience to the second commandment and name the Absolute. Adorno named 'Nonpossessive devotion'. But for Adorno, this utopian quality is purely immanent, a potential attribute of human love in a perfect society. There is no God whose relation to his creatures can only be described as 'non-possessive devotion'.

Nevertheless, there are theologians who find here the key to a theology that can pass through the Feuerbachian purgatory, the Marxian critique and the Freudian enlightenment. Peukert, followed by Siebert, finds in the ideal of non-possessive devotion the core of a theological anthropology and a political theology on the premiss that such a quality of human relations only makes sense and is preserved from futility if it is grounded in a transcendent personal reality that inspires all authentic liberating human intercourse and sustains eternally the values it reflects. There is a God whose non-possessive devotion towards his creation means that he underwrites, preserves, rescues and redeems all acts and intentions of non-possessive devotion within humanity. No true love is wasted, no longing for liberty unfulfilled, no cry for deliverance ultimately unanswered. The murderer shall indeed not triumph everlastingly over his innocent victim. As Siebert says of Adorno's naming of the Absolute:

> This name indicates the theological glowing fire in historical materialism. This name constitutes the connection between theology and dialectical materialism. This name is the key to the theodicy problem. This name signifies the very core of a critical political theology which can inspire anamnestic as well as proleptic solidarity. (Siebert 1985, p. 369)

Talk of inter-personal devotion notwithstanding, the social dimension of critical theory is actually rather attenuated. The critical theorist retains the Enlightenment ideal of the courageous individual daring to use his reason in defiance of enthroned authority – yet without the hubris of the Enlightenment. As Connerton puts it:

> The critical theorist seeks discharge from the responsibility which the Enlightenment claim to autonomy has enjoined upon him . . . In the Frankfurt School the aspirations of the Enlightenment remain but its illusions have been lost . . . Critical theory is the Achilles heel of the Enlightenment brought to light. (p. 119)

The vocation of the critical theorist is the 'melancholy' one alluded to in the title of Gillian Rose's study. The critical theorist does not have faith that non-oppressive communities can be created and in which he can find a home. The critical theorist remains on the margin, the 'prophet without honour'.

If the remedy of critical theory lacks social substance, that may well be because the diagnosis also lacks it. As Connerton has pointed out (ch. 4), Horkheimer and Adorno neglect the whole social formation of the individual and are weak on the intersubjective dimension of experience. Now religion is a collective phenomenon or it is nothing. The substance of religious faith and practice emerges when at least 'two or three are gathered together'. Liturgy, sacraments, ministry and service, by definition, cannot occur for the isolated individual. Faith cannot be handed on except in tradition. It is typically when believers are 'all with one accord in one place' (Acts 2. 1) that the spirit moves.

Durkheim et al.

It was the genius of Émile Durkheim to have recognized this. For Durkheim, religion and society, though not convertible, were inextricably linked. 'If religion has given birth to all that is essential in society,' he wrote in *The Elementary Forms of the Religious Life*, 'it is because the idea of society is the soul of religion' (p. 419). Durkheim's view, that religion can be accounted for by its social function, is, like Marx's or Freud's, a reductionist account of religion. As a nineteenth-century rationalist *par excellence*, Durkheim did not believe in any transcendent being who was creator and redeemer. But Durkheim stands apart from the thoroughgoing reductionists in so far as he does not regard religion as pathological, an aberration, a symptom of social or personal sickness, destined to wither away. Religion is not dismissed as illusion. 'Our entire study,' he insists at the conclusion of his *magnum opus*, 'rests upon this postulate that the unanimous sentiment of the believers of all times cannot be purely illusory' (p. 417). Religion has an ultimately cognitive function, though not a veridical one. 'Feasts and rites', he insists, 'are not the whole of religion.'

This is not merely a system of practices, but also a

system of ideas whose object is to explain the world . . .
even the humblest have their cosmology . . . [There are]
two elements of the religious life . . . The one is turned
towards action, which it demands and regulates; the
other is turned towards thought, which it enriches and
organises. (p. 428)

The sociologist Robert Bellah and the anthropologist Clif-
ford Geertz are working in the Durkheimian tradition when
they take religious symbols as – paradoxically – cognitive but
not veridical. Theologians have been over-hasty in appealing
to Bellah's notion of 'symbolic realism' in support of theological realism. When Bellah says, 'To put it bluntly, religion
is true,' he means merely that religion is, as Durkheim
claimed, *sui generis*, and cannot be reduced to psychological
or sociological residues. It means that, 'since religious sym-
bolisation and religious experience are inherent in the structure of human existence, all reductionism must be
abandoned.' But religious symbols remain 'noncognitive' by
which Bellah seems to mean that they do not refer to an
objective reality. 'I am certainly not supporting the claims of
the historical realist theologians who are still working with a
cognitive conception of religious belief that makes it parallel
to objectivist scientific description' (Bellah, pp. 124–6).

Geertz, similarly, in his well-known essay on religion as
a cultural system, emphasises the explanatory intention of
religious symbols. One of their functions is to 'synthesise a
people's . . . world view – the picture they have of the way
things in actuality are, their most comprehensive ideas of
order'. Religious symbols contain a specific – though usually
implicit – metaphysic. Their job is to make that interpretation
of reality convincing. They clothe metaphysical concepts
'with such an aura of factuality' that the moods and motivations inculcated by the symbols 'seem uniquely realistic'
(Geertz, pp. 89f). In a further essay, Geertz makes it clear
that the claim of religions to make objective statements about
cosmic order is only apparent: a religious symbols structure
merely 'seems to mediate genuine knowledge'; it gives only
'an appearance of objectivity'. His assessment of the cognitive
claims of religions is profoundly relativistic: 'What all sacred
symbols assert is that the good for man is to live realistically;

where they differ is in the vision of reality they construct' (Geertz, pp. 129–31).

Though they flirt with the notion of realism, Bellah and Geertz are still reductionists at heart. Contrary to appearances, they persist with a non-realist view of religious symbols. The emphasis on cosmic meaning and value contained in religious symbols, emphasised by Durkheim, Bellah and Geertz, is also a major feature of Peter Berger's work in the framework of the sociology of knowledge. But, as is well known, Berger leaves open the possibility that there is actually an objective correlative to those symbols – God.

Sociology of Knowledge

It is the self-appointed task of the discipline of the sociology of knowledge to investigate the dynamics of how we create our picture of reality, to portray the sources, modes, structures and patterns of the social construction of our world. The sociology of knowledge points us to that never-ceasing human activity of pouring out meaning into reality by projection as the way we build 'a humanly meaningful world' (Berger 1973, p. 36). Projection results in objectification as the content of what is projected on to the screen of the phenomenal world assumes 'objective' existence. Through constant repetition ('habitualisation') this gives rise to various social institutions which are now the focus of our shared projections. Those institutions now take on a life of their own, generating that activity of self-maintenance and protection which we call legitimation. Legitimation is the function of demonstrating why things are as they are and why they should remain that way. The result is a complete 'symbolic universe', an emotionally, intellectually and morally satisfying home for the human spirit. As Berger and Luckmann put it:

> As man externalises himself, he constructs the world *into* which he externalises himself. In the process of externalisation, he projects his own meanings into reality. Symbolic universes, which proclaim that *all* reality is humanly meaningful and call upon the *entire* cosmos to signify the validity of human existence, constitute the furthest reaches of this projection. (p. 122)

As we have already seen, the highest, most ambitious and most sophisticated expression of this process constitutes the religious activity of mankind. All religious reflection, including prayer, worship and preaching contributes to the creation of the symbolic universe of a particular religious tradition, but the task of institutionalisation and legitimation falls to the various departments of theology. Berger defines religion as 'the establishment, through human activity, of an all-embracing sacred order, that is, of a sacred cosmos that will be capable of maintaining itself in the ever-present face of chaos' (1973, p. 59). Certainly, all projection contains a tacit metaphysical thrust. Whether it is political policies or ethical choices that are being considered, we need to feel that they are not arbitrary and *ad hoc*, but somehow conform to 'the way things are'. But in the religious construction of reality this cosmic, metaphysical reference becomes explicit. It assumes the importance of a *raison d'être* that undergirds those particular, local and temporal matters where we are still struggling for the realisation of an ideal. As Hans Möl puts it, it is 'the projection of meaning and order into a transcendent point of reference where the essences and archetypes of the mundane can be made to appear more orderly, consistent and timeless' (p. 241).

At this point there are a couple of qualifications that need to be made. First, to say that a religious worldview is socially *created* is not the same as saying that it is socially *determined*, that it is merely the shadow or echo of social processes. Though Marx does give the impression that this is what he means, it is emphatically disavowed by Berger, for example. 'It is *not* implied,' Berger insists, 'that any particular religious system is nothing but the effect or "reflection" of social processes. Rather, the point is that the *same* human activity that produces society also produces religion' (1973, p. 56). Religion is a human activity; theology is a human activity: the outstanding question therefore is, where does *divine* activity come in, if anywhere? To attempt an answer to this question would take us beyond the scope of this book, which is attempting the limited task of neutralising the reductionist veto which would have it that Christian claims to a transcendent, divine objective reality are reducible to human projections without remainder.

The second qualification concerns the relation between social processes and intellectual activity. Once again, where Marx seems to imply a one-sided influence of social and economic conditions on the formation of ideas (which are thus constituted as ideology), sociologists of knowledge are both more cautious and more realistic. The relationship between ideas and 'their sustaining social processes', Berger and Luckmann maintain, is always dialectical. 'It is correct to say that theories are concocted in order to legitimate already existing social institutions. But it also happens that social institutions are changed in order to bring them into conformity with already existing theories, that is, to make them more "legitimate" ' (p. 145). Both idealistic and materialistic interpretations of the relation between society and ideology distort its dialectical nature (p. 146). This certainly supports the hope that ecclesiastical policies and practices are not entirely at the mercy of the interests they represent, but may be susceptible to reform and correction in the light of theological theories. But for those theories to be acceptable it would be essential for them to show that they are expressions of the Church's 'true nature', of her original mandate, or of the 'essence' of Christianity.

8

The Reductionist Veto Vetoed

Surely there exists somewhere,
as the justification of our looking for it,
the one light that can cast such shadows?

(R. S. THOMAS, p. 73)

I set out at the beginning of this short book to study half a dozen of the most unsparing modern critics of Christianity. I wanted to face up to the most damning things that have been said about the Christian faith. I purposed to ask myself to what extent these criticisms are justified, and, where they carry conviction, how they might be remedied. We recall that the thinkers studied here, with the possible exception of Jung (whose relation to Christianity, as we have seen, was ambiguous), believed that they had invalidated Christian belief in principle; they had cut at the very root; they had shown that the belief in God was an illusion caused by the projection of individual and social struggles.

It gives pause for thought that some of the greatest seminal thinkers of modern times, whose thought has shaken the world – Marx, Nietzsche and Freud – have been implacably hostile to Christianity. At the same time I have been impressed, as I have glanced at their biographical background, with their profound humanity, their struggles, sufferings and aspirations. I have learned to respect and admire them. I have learned a good deal from them. I wonder now, at the end of this study, whether, as a result of their strictures, the Christian faith is irredeemably and irretrievably condemned, or whether the hostility of these thinkers was directed merely at distortions and corruptions of the true nature of Christianity, which can then emerge purified and strengthened.

One factor to be weighed is that none of those studied here were ignorant of religion. They were not speaking of what they did not know. They were not imagining an illusory foe, tilting at windmills. All had had formative contact with religion.

- Feuerbach had studied theology and had sat at the feet of Hegel and Schleiermacher. His *The Essence of Christianity* shows a thorough grasp of Christian doctrine.
- Marx was descended on his father's side from a line of rabbis and his orthodox Jewish mother attempted to keep Jewish observances going in the household. As a young student Marx was filled with a fervent Protestant piety like that of the young Schleiermacher.
- Nietzsche was the son and grandson of Lutheran pastors. He was brought up in an atmosphere of warm feminine piety. His youthful poems express heartfelt devotion to Christ.
- Freud never renounced his Jewish racial identity. He identified with Joseph and Moses. His Roman Catholic nurse took him to visit the churches and her Catholicism made an indelible impression on the young Freud.
- Jung had eight uncles who were parsons and his own father was a Reformed minister. Jung was nurtured in parsonage and parish. He had acquainted himself with his father's library, included Reformed dogmatics. He had a thorough knowledge of the Bible and a good grasp of doctrine. Like Freud, Jung made a biblical figure central to his thought: *Answer to Job* is probably his best known work.

Let me set out now several points by way of a critical evaluation of the reductionist approach as we find it in the thinkers whom we have studied, before going on to make a substantial proposal about the 'reductionist veto'.

First, the reductionists prove too much. Few would be prepared to go all the way with the more extreme reductionists. Feuerbach's reduction of theology began with his exposure of philosophy as an esoteric form of the knowledge of humanity expressed in mystifying abstractions. Nietzsche deconstructed not only Christian theology but all rational epistemology, metaphysics, ethics and aesthetics. He dismissed Socrates as 'rabble'. The New Testament made him retch. We travel Nietzsche's road at peril not only of our faith but of our sanity.

Second, their interpretations of Christianity – and hence their criticisms – are often wide of the mark. Feuerbach insisted against the more enlightened theologians of his time that Christians worship an angry God. He would not allow his caricature to be challenged. Nietzsche blamed St Paul for the sick legacy of Christianity which he regarded as anti-life, just as he blamed Socrates for the legacy of Western philosophy. Even at its most patriarchal and ascetic, and for all its appalling shortcomings in its treatment of women, Christianity has taught that the physical is God's good creation, that sexuality is part of God's plan and that our desires are 'implanted by God'. It is plain false to claim with Marx that Christianity is inherently and inescapably on the side of privilege and oppression, even though its record in this respect is hardly a shining one.

Third, these thinkers were implacable in their rejection of the institutional Church. Marx saw it as synonymous with bourgeois capitalist privilege. Nietzsche blamed the Church, not Jesus of Nazareth, for the evils of Christianity: its cruelty, obscurantism and hostility to life, desire and beauty. Freud, though terrorised by the Nazis, held that his greatest enemy was actually the Roman Catholic Church. Jung had night-mares about sinister black-garbed ecclesiastical figures, held most clergy in contempt and believed that the Church was beyond enlightenment. As we have seen, he had some grounds in his experience for this jaundiced view. The reductionists are our allies in working for the continual reform of the institutional Church; their bad experiences are no excuse for us to abandon it.

Fourth, the atheism of the reductionists (not Jung) was not a conclusion that emerged from their argument or a convic-tion forced upon them by their researches. Feuerbach, Marx, Nietzsche and Freud had all rejected the Christian faith and lost their belief in God before they embarked on their great projects. Atheism is not necessarily entailed in Feuerbach's use of the concept of projection, Marx's analysis of class conflict or Freud's method of psychoanalysis.

Fifth, they saw through the spurious objectivity of tra-ditional Christian theology which held that divine revelation was objectively embodied in the Bible and Church teachings without impairment from the human, social and historical channels through which it had to pass. These masters of suspicion knew that there is no route to objectivity that does not pass through subjectivity with all its wiles, pretences and distortions. The pioneer explorers of the unconscious, Freud and Jung – and should we not include Nietzsche here? – knew that the vast ocean of subjectivity could not be ignored. It actually held the key to knowledge. The reductionist critique of Christianity in the nineteenth century represents the revenge of the subject.

Sixth, however, their conclusion that Christian belief was a great delusional system created out of human subjectivity, did not necessarily follow. It is possible, as Kierkegaard showed, to take our subjectivity with radical seriousness without reductionism. There is a sense in which Kierkegaard endorses Feuerbach's dictum that 'God is the highest subjectivity of man.' While the reductionists insist that the turn to the subject is a turning away from God and belief, the passionately believing Kierkegaard also holds that 'truth is subjectivity'.

Seventh, the reductionists believed that once they had exposed the psychological mechanism of projection, and shown how beliefs arose, they had disposed of the validity of religious faith. Nietzsche's triumphant exposé of the origin of religion is a classic example of the genetic fallacy. Freud, who also brings out the aetiology of religious belief and practice, was compelled to admit that this did not entail consequences for the truth or falsity of religious teachings. The reductionists did not entertain the possibility that Christian theology could cope with the fact of projection, that it could admit it into its interpretation of the mystery of divine-human relations – the dynamic of revelation and its reception, the inseparable conjunction of human discovery and divine self-disclosure. This point deserves separate consideration at greater length and leads into the substance of our conclusion.

The reductionist challenge to Christianity asserts that the essence of Christianity is nothing but a projection of the psycho-social essence of humanity. If the truth of Christianity is to be affirmed, the reductionist veto must be disposed of first. To do this, it is not necessary to demonstrate positively that there *is* an objective, transcendent, divine reality that reveals itself to mankind. That constructive task falls to the disciplines of the philosophy of religion, natural theology and, above all, fundamental theology (apologetics). In modern theology, Rahner and Pannenberg are notably successful exponents of this approach (cf. Avis, 1986c). It is only necessary to show that the reductionist case remains 'not proven'. Peter Berger calls this 'relativising the relativisers': I call it 'the reductionist veto vetoed'. We have already seen that it is justifiable to regard individual irrational fears and social paranoia as projections of unresolved problems on to external dark forces. But is it also acceptable to regard our hopes, aspirations and ideals as projected on to external beneficient forces, in other words, on to 'God'?

The Neapolitan philosopher Giambattista Vico was the first to combine early in the eighteenth century, a fully relativistic historical method with a belief in divine providence and revelation. Vico sees the phenomenon of projection as the means employed by a merciful providence to reveal itself to humanity. In the purely immanent processes of the struggle of primitive people for survival, the reality of divine providence came to be revealed. In his account of the origins of Gentile religion (he tactfully steered clear of the biblical revelation which was protected by ecclesiastical and civil sanctions), Vico speculated that, as Noah's Flood appeared, the most robust of the race of giants who lived among the wild beasts in the great forests of the mountains, were compelled to lift their eyes from earth to heaven.

> And because in such a case the nature of the human mind leads it to attribute its own nature to the effect . . . they pictured the sky to themselves as a great animated body . . . And thus they began to exercise that natural curiosity which is the daughter of ignorance and the mother of knowledge, and which, opening the mind of man, gives birth to wonder. (Vico, p. 377ff)

It was thus that the first religions were born:

> The first theological poets created the first divine fable, the greatest they ever created: that of Jove, king and father of men and Gods, in the act of hurling the light-

ning bolt; an image so popular, disturbing and instruc-
tive that its creators themselves believed in it and feared,
revered and worshipped it in frightful religions. (ibid.)

Wonder led to worship and worship to beliefs and practices,
particularly marriage and burial rites. Thus, Vico concludes,
'through the thick clouds of those first tempests, intermittently lit by those [lightning] flashes, they made out this great
truth: that divine providence watches over the welfare of all
mankind' (ibid. para. 385; Avis, 1986b, p. 149).

Surely the whole point about projection is that there is
something to project on to? We project inner stereotypes (or
as Jung would say, archetypes) on to real people to form
certain essential relationships. We project subjective meaning
on to real social structures. No one seriously suggests that
other selves and social reality are figments of our imagination.
Similarly we project transcendent symbols and ideals on to a
real transcendent reality. There is something there that evokes
our response. But that response is the only sort we are capable
of, the imaging of that reality in terms of our highest and
noblest ideals. How could it be otherwise? As John Bowker
has pointed out: 'A world of the gods, to be plausible, must
have at least some features which men can imaginatively
identify. Jerusalem on high may have streets of gold, but they
are at least streets; God may have a voice like thunder, but
he has at least a voice' (p. 30). The human sciences can shed
light on the social patterns of projection, its morphology, but
they cannot explain its ultimate dynamism, its origin, what
impels it. As Bowker says, 'We are not studying massive
mechanisms of social process, or of individuation, alone, in
which it is virtually irrelevant what objects are or are not
encountered – as though the mechanism will in any case run
on.' The human sciences must take account of the contribu-
tory effect of the putative objects of encounter, thus leaving
open the possibility that the origin of the sense of God may
be – God (p. 181; cf. 16).

But I am not entirely convinced by Bowker when he
claims, in criticism of Berger's approach, that there may be
'access to realities in existence which are independent of that
cultural relativity which is undoubtedly the foundation of
[our] gaining access to anything . . . the possibility cannot be

excluded that men draw on resources of meaning which exist apart from the social.' Bowker therefore holds out the possibility that there might be 'a sufficiency of reality in existence in the external universe for there to be a groundwork of perception' which would form a basis for constructing an interpretation of objective reality (pp. 33f). Bowker's objection to Berger (1973) is that he does not fully reckon with the possibility that, while we pour meaning into our environment, that environment ('that which is externally the case') may be pouring meaning into us (p. 37). Although he eschews any kind of 'man of the gaps' approach (by analogy with the god of the gaps accommodation of science and theology), which would find objectivity in some loophole in the network of scientific explanation (p. 19), it seems that Bowker has not fully succeeded in resisting the temptation to find a way of bypassing human projections. It is not the existence of a transcendent reality that I question, but the implied suggestion that there may be modes of perception, routes of access to them that escape the gravitational pull of social relativity.

Here I am in agreement with Berger when he deplores any 'search for religious phenomena that will somehow manifest themselves as different from human projections.' As Berger rightly insists: 'Nothing is immune to the relativisation of socio-historical analysis. Whatever else these phenomena may be, they will *also* be human projections, products of human history, social constructions undertaken by human beings' (1971, p. 65). For Berger personally this does not exclude the possibility that 'in, with and under' (ibid.) these projections the echo of a communication from a transcendent, objective reality may be detected. In his later book *The Heretical Imperative* this possibility is affirmed more strongly: 'Religion can be understood as a human projection because it is communicated in human symbols. But this very communication is motivated by an experience in which a metahuman reality is injected into human life' (1980, p. 52). To illustrate this paradox, Berger offers an analogy: travellers returning from a far country with tales of what they have seen. Let it be assumed that every one of their accounts can be shown to be shaped by the historical, socio-economic and psychological characteristics of the traveller in question. 'As the critical observer analyses all these reports, it is perfectly plausible for him to perceive the faraway country as a gigantic projection of the travellers' own country.' But the irreducible fact remains that they have been there and can tell us something about it (pp. 122f).

I see no reason, therefore, to regard the verdict of the human sciences that all religion is a psycho-social projection as reductionist in any pejorative or destructive sense. It certainly does not deal a death blow to religion. It only reminds us – and Christianity above all should not need reminding – that religion is a human activity. Shelley spoke in *Prometheus Unbound* of 'all that faith creates or love desires' (p. 219). As Marx insists, 'Man makes religion, religion does not make man.' We cannot get behind the veil of that activity to peer at transcendent reality as it 'really' is. This conclusion does however entail consequences for a doctrine of revelation: it means that we do not enjoy any privileged, unmediated, wholly objective communication from God. But that is not news to any enlightened Christian theology. It means that, instead of postulating a sphere of divine communication ('revelation') and a separate sphere of human response ('reason'), we should learn to operate in terms of an integrated realm of 'the sacred' in which divine disclosure and human projection are distinguishable only hypothetically. Revelation remains an all-essential postulate – religion would not make sense without it – but nevertheless it remains a postulate; you cannot put your finger on it; you cannot say, *this* is revelation but *that* is human response.

All religion, without exception – and that means without exception for the prophetic 'thus saith the Lord', or the papal *ex cathedra* pronouncement, or even the *ipsissima verba* of our Lord Jesus Christ – is human projection and reflects social and psychological processes. But I cannot believe that this is to evacuate religion of its transcendent reference, any more than it is reductionist to understand creation in terms of evolution, providence in terms of second causes and inspiration in terms of advancing spiritual insight. In every case, the sustaining, salvific presence of God is mediated through natural mundane or human processes and is discernible to the eyes of faith in, with and under them.

If, as Vico suggested, the origins of morality and religion

can be discovered, by a strenuous effort of empathetic insight, in primitive humanity's instinctive response to the crashing of thunder in the mountains, surely the seeds of our most elevated conceptions of goodness, beauty and love can be traced without shame to the satisfying of the infant's craving for nourishment at its mother's breast? The God whose supreme revelation, according to the Christian faith, is found in a new-born baby, would, presumably, not disdain such humble and homely methods to teach us the love of God. The one who, according to the Christian story, was born in a stable and laid in a manger, would not refuse to become implicated in the sometimes sordid processes of individual psychological development and social struggle with its compelling drives and often crude projections.

Moreover, it seems to me that to come to terms with this possibility, far from disposing of Christianity as a credible faith, actually results in a faith that is more subtle, more sophisticated, purged of infantile fantasies, and an adult proposition in a tough intellectual world. In postulating a sublime act of divine humility, condescension and 'kenosis', this interpretation leads us close to the heart of the Christian mystery which is essentially incarnational. In this way, it may well be that Feuerbach's river of fire may be transmuted into Auden's affirming flame.

If this is so, then Christian theology needs to hear the remorseless critique of the modern unbelievers, even though their message may be disturbing and unwelcome. Though we cannot allow their reductionist veto, they have much to say that can purify and refine our vision of the Christian mystery. In the mystical tradition, an essential preparation for the unitive path, which is the ultimate destination of the spirit, is the way of purgation, in which the soul is stripped of all pretensions, illusions and tricks of self-deception, and is thus prepared for its encounter with God. Thinkers like Horkheimer and Adorno, who worked in the shadow of fascism, total war and the holocaust, are like secular mystics journeying the purgative way. Employing both Marxist and Freudian critique in an abrasive kind of psycho-social therapy they offer us their bleak enlightenment in a world that seems to have almost forgotten God. They are perhaps the 'ironic points of light' of which Auden spoke in 'September 1 1939', that flash out their coded signals in the darkness of 'negation and despair'. That kind of critique is, no doubt, a necessary stage, a penitential moment, a Lenten fast, a purgative way, a journey into the desert.

Nietzsche once urged Christians to enter voluntarily the wilderness of unbelief for a while – only so could they win the right to continue to believe:

> These serious, excellent, upright, deeply sensitive people who are still Christians from the very heart: they owe it to themselves to try for once the experiment of living for some length of time without Christianity; they owe it to *their faith* in this way for once to sojourn 'in the wilderness' – if only to win for themselves the right to a voice on the question whether Christianity is necessary.(*D*, p. 37: para. 61)

But these John the Baptist figures may become the unwitting heralds of a coming one whose enlightenment is more radiant than theirs, more warming, more cheering, more healing, more life-giving. They may serve unsuspectingly to prepare the way – precisely in the desert – for the revealing of the presence of God in Christ, by purifying the Church and its theology so that it may become more transparent to the gospel of Christ. As Karl Rahner has written, in Jesus 'we see a human being whose life is characterised by an unsurpassable nearness to God. It is a life of absolute obedience to God and at the same time of unconditional solidarity with the human race... This twofold solidarity with God and with humankind is sustained by Jesus unconditionally' through death and into resurrection (*TI*, 21, p. 216).

By the power of his own definitive awareness of God, the wholeness of his humanity (cf. Schleiermacher, pp. 385ff, 425ff), Jesus continually subverts, calls in question and overthrows all distortions of ideology. He is, in Christian belief, both the definitive symbol of selfhood and the definitive symbol of God. In him we see the union of humanity and deity. He is the greater healer of humanity's identity. Amid all the constraints under which Christian theology is compelled to operate in the modern context, the retrenchments and retractions forced by the fires of criticism, redemption can still be experienced through the gospel, adoration can still set our hearts on fire. To conclude, as we began, with Auden (p. 143):

> In the deserts of the heart
> Let the healing fountain start,
> In the prison of his days
> Teach the free man how to praise.

A Speculative Postscript

At the end of his extraordinary fantasy of the unconscious and its symbols, *Lilith*, George MacDonald has the narrator ask,

'Could God himself create such lovely things as I dreamed?'
'Whence then comes thy dream,' answers Hope.
'Out of my dark self, into the light of my consciousness.'
'But whence first into thy dark self?' rejoins Hope.
'My brain was its mother, and the fever in my blood its father.'
'Say rather,' suggests Hope, 'thy brain was the violin whence it issued and the fever in thy blood the bow that drew it forth. But who made the violin? and who guided the bow across its strings? . . . Whence came the Fantasia? and whence the life that danced thereto? . . .'

MacDonald adds the reflection: 'Man dreams and desires; God broods and wills and quickens. When a man dreams his own dream, he is the sport of his dream; when Another gives it him, the Other is able to fulfil it.' He brings his work to an end by quoting the romantic poet Novalis: 'Our life is no dream, but it should and will perhaps become one.'

Bibliography

Adorno, T. W. 1967. *Prisms*. London, Spearman.

Adorno, T. W. 1973. *Negative Dialectics*. London, Routledge & Kegan Paul.

Adorno, T. W. 1974. *Minima Moralia: Reflections from Damaged Life*. London, NLB/Verso.

Adorno, T. W. 1977. 'The Actuality of Philosophy', *Telos*, 31 (1977), pp. 120–33.

Appleton, G. 1985. *The Oxford Book of Prayer*. Oxford, Oxford University Press.

Aquinas, T. *S.T. Summa Theologiae*. London, Eyre & Spottiswoode; New York, McGraw-Hill (1964).

Arato, A., and Gebhardt, E. (eds.) 1978. *The Essential Frankfurt School Reader*. Oxford, Basil Blackwell.

Auden, W. H. 1969. *Collected Shorter Poems 1927–1957*. London, Faber & Faber.

Avis, P. D. L. 1982. 'In the Shadow of the Frankfurt School: From "Critical Theory" to "Critical Theology" ', *Scottish Journal of Theology*, 35 (1982), pp. 529–40.

Avis, P. D. L. 1986a. *Ecumenical Theology and the Elusiveness of Doctrine*. London, SPCK, and Cambridge Mass., Cowley (*Truth Beyond Words*).

Avis, P. D. L. 1986b. *Foundations of Modern Historical Thought: From Machiavelli to Vico*. London, Croom Helm.

Avis, P. D. L. 1986c. *The Methods of Modern Theology*. Basingstoke, Marshall Pickering.

Avis, P. D. L. (ed.) 1988. *Threshold of Theology*. Basingstoke, Marshall Pickering.

Avis, P. D. L. 1989. *Eros and the Sacred*. London, SPCK, and Wilton Conn., Morehouse-Barlow, 1990.

Avis, P. D. L. 1992. *Authority, Leadership and Conflict in the Church*. London, Mowbray, and New York, Trinity Press International.

Bacon, F. 1890. *Essays*. London, Macmillan.

Bacon, F. 1905. *Philosophical Works*. Ed., J. M. Robertson. London, Routledge.

Bacon, F. 1915. *Of the Advancement of Learning*. London, Dent.

Bacon, F. 1964. *The Philosophy of Francis Bacon*. Ed. B. Farrington. Liverpool, Liverpool University Press.

Barth, K. 1972. *Protestant Theology in the Nineteenth Century*. London, SCM Press.

Barth, K. *CD. Church Dogmatics*. Ed. T. F. Torrance and G. W. Bromiley. Edinburgh, T & T Clark, 1956.

Baumeister, R. F. 1986. *Identity: Cultural Change and the Struggle for Self*. New York, Oxford University Press.

Beer, J. 1986. 'Did Lamb understand Coleridge?' *The Charles Lamb Bulletin*. N. S. 56.

Bellah, R. N. 1987. 'Theology and Symbolic Realism', in R. Gill (ed.), *Theology and Sociology: A Reader*. London, Geoffrey Chapman, and New York, Paulist Press.

Berger, P. 1971. *A Rumour of Angels*. Harmondsworth, Penguin.

Berger, P. 1973. *The Social Reality of Religion*. Harmondsworth, Penguin (USA: *The Sacred Canopy*).

Berger, P. 1980. *The Heretical Imperative*. London, Collins.

Berger, P. and Luckmann, T. 1967. *The Social Construction of Reality*. London, Allen Lane, The Penguin Press.

Bernstein, R. J., 1972. *Praxis and Action*. London, Duckworth, and Philadelphia, University of Philadelphia Press, 1971.

Bettelheim, B. 1985. *Freud and Man's Soul*. London, Flamingo.

Bowker, J. 1973. *The Sense of God*. Oxford, Clarendon Press.

Bridges, R. 1929. *The Testament of Beauty*. Oxford, Clarendon Press.

Brome, V. 1978. *Jung: Man and Myth*. St. Albans, Granada.

Buck-Morss, S. 1977. *The Origin of Negative Dialectics*. Sussex, Harvester Press.

Calvin, J. n.d. *Institutes of the Christian Religion*. London, J. Clarke.

Clark, R. W. 1982. *Freud: The Man and the Cause*. London, Granada.

Connerton, P. 1980. *The Tragedy of Enlightenment*. Cambridge, Cambridge University Press.

Conquest, R. 1988. *New and Collected Poems*. London, Hutchinson.

Copleston, F. 1965. *A History of Philosophy: 7, Schopenhauer to Nietzsche.* New York, Image.

Dante, 1981. *The Divine Comedy.* trans. C. H. Sisson, London, Pan.

Durkheim, E. 1915. *The Elementary Forms of the Religious Life.* Trans. J. W. Swain, London, Allen & Unwin.

Eliot, T. S. 1974. *Collected Poems 1909–1962.* London, Faber & Faber.

Erikson, E. 1968. *Identity: Youth and Crisis.* London, Faber & Faber.

Erikson, E. 1977. *Childhood and Society.* London, Paladin.

Feenberg, A. 1981. *Lukács, Marx and The Sources of Critical Theory.* Oxford, Robertson.

Ferenczi, S. 1952. 'Transference and Introjection', in *First Contributions to Psychoanalysis.* Ed. and trans. E. Jones, London, Hogarth.

Feuerbach, L. 1957. *The Essence of Christianity.* Trans. G. Eliot, New York, Harper.

Feuerbach, L. 1967. *Lectures on the Essence of Religion.* Trans. R. Manheim, New York, Harper & Row.

Forsyth, J. 1989. *Freud, Jung and Christianity.* Ottawa, Ottawa University Press.

Foucault, M. 1986. *The Foucault Reader.* Ed. P. Rabinsov, Harmondsworth, Penguin.

Freud, S. *PFL. Pelican Freud Library.* Harmondsworth, Penguin.

Freud and Pfister see Meng, H. and Freud, E. L. (eds.).

Fromm, E. 1980. *Beyond the Chains of Illusion.* London, Sphere.

Gay, P. 1987. *A Godless Jew: Freud, Atheism and the Making of Psychoanalysis.* New Haven and London, Yale University Press.

Geertz, C. 1973. *The Interpretation of Cultures.* New York, Basic Books.

Geuss, R. 1981. *The Idea of a Critical Theory.* Cambridge, Cambridge University Press.

Goethe, J. W. von, 1971. *Elective Affinities.* Trans. R. J. Hollingdale, Harmondsworth, Penguin.

Guntrip, H. 1977. *Personality Structure and Human Interaction.* London, Hogarth.

Habermas, J. 1972. *Knowledge and Human Interests.* London, Heinemann.

Harvey, V. A. 1985. 'Ludwig Feuerbach and Karl Marx', in Smart, Clayton, Katz and Sherry (eds.), *Nineteenth Century Religious Thought in the West,* 1. Cambridge, Cambridge University Press.

Held, D. 1980. *Introduction to Critical Theory: Horkheimer to Habermas.* London, Hutchinson.

Hook, S. 1936. *From Hegel to Marx.* London, Gollancz.

Horkheimer, M. 1941. 'The End of Reason', *Zeitzschrift fur Sozialforschung.* 9 (1941), pp. 366–88.

Horkheimer, M. 1972. *Critical Theory: Selected Essays*. New York, Seabury.

Horkheimer, M. 1974. *Eclipse of Reason*. New York, Seabury.

Horkheimer, M. and Adorno, T. W. 1973. *Dialectic of Enlightenment*. London, Allen Lane, Penguin Press.

Horkheimer, M. and Adorno, T. W. (eds.) 1973. *Aspects of Sociology*. London, Heinemann.

Hume, D. 1875. *Essays: Moral, Political and Literary* 2. Ed. T. H. Green and T. H. Grose, London.

Jay, M. 1973. *The Dialectic Imagination: A History of the Frankfurt School and the Institute of Social Research 1923–1950*. London, Heinemann.

Jay, M. 1984a. *Adorno*. London, Fount.

Jay, M. 1984b. *Marxism and Totality*. Berkeley, University of California Press.

Jung, C. G. 1973. *Letters*. Ed. G. Adler, London, Routledge & Kegan Paul.

Jung, C. G. 1983a. *Memories, Dreams, Reflections*. London, Flamingo.

Jung, C. G. 1983b. *The Psychology of the Transference*. London, Ark.

Jung, C. G. 1984. *Answer to Job*. London, Ark.

Jung, C. G. 1985. *Dreams*. London, Ark.

Jung, C. G. *SW. Selected Works*. Ed. A. Storr. London, Fontana, 1983.

Jung, C. G. *CW. Collected Works*. London, Routledge & Kegan Paul, 1954.

Jung, C. G. n.d. *Aspects of the Feminine*. London, Ark.

Kaufman, W. 1965. *Hegel*. London, Weidenfeld and Nicholson.

Kaufman, W. 1968. *Nietzsche*. Princeton NJ, Princeton University Press.

Kee, A. 1990. *Marx and the Failure of Liberation Theology*. London, SCM Press, and Philadelphia, TPI.

Kerr, F. 1986. *Theology After Wittgenstein*. Oxford, Basil Blackwell.

Kolakowski, L. 1978. *Main Currents of Marxism, 1, The Founders*. Oxford, Clarendon Press.

Küng, H. 1990 (1979). *Freud and the Problem of God* (enlarged edn). New Haven and London, Yale University Press.

Küng, H. 1980. *Does God Exist?*. London, Collins.

Lash, N. L. A. 1981. *A Matter of Hope*. London, Darton, Longman & Todd.

Lash, N. L. A. 1986. *Theology on the Way to Emmaus*. London, SCM Press.

Lasswell, H. G. 1951. *Psychopathology and Politics*, in *The Writings of H. D. Lasswell*. Glencoe, Free Press.

Lee, R. S. 1948. *Freud and Christianity*. London, Clarke.

Lukács, G. 1971. *History and Class Consciousness*. London, Merlin Press.

Luther, M. *WA. D. Martin Luthers Werke*. Weimarer Ausgabe, Weimar, 1883–1982.

MacDonald, G. 1964. *Phantastes and Lilith*. Grand Rapids, Mich., Eerdmans.

McKown, D. B. 1975. *The Classical Marxist Critique of Religion: Marx, Engels, Lenin, Kautsky*. The Hague, Nijhoff.

McLellan, D. 1969. *The Young Hegelians and Karl Marx*. London, Macmillan.

McLellan, D. 1976. *Karl Marx: His Life and Thought*. London, Paladin.

McLellan, D. 1987. *Marxism and Religion*. Basingstoke, Macmillan.

Marx, K. 1972. *Karl Marx: Early Texts*. Ed. D. McLellan. Oxford, Basil Blackwell.

Marx, K. and Engels, F. 1965. *The German Ideology*. London, Lawrence and Wishart.

Meissner, W. W. 1984. *Psychoanalysis and Religious Experience*. New Haven, Yale University Press.

Meng, H., and Freud, E. L. (eds.), 1963. *Sigmund Freud and Oskar Pfister*. London, Hogarth.

Milbank, J. 1990. *Theology and Social Theory*. Oxford, Basil Blackwell.

Mol, H. 1976. *Identity and the Sacred*. Oxford, Basil Blackwell.

Moore, R. L. and Meckel, D. J. (eds). 1990. *Jung and Christianity in Dialogue*. New York, Paulist Press.

Nagy, M. 1991. *Philosophical Issues in the Psychology of C. G. Jung*. New York, State University of New York Press.

Nelson, B. (ed.). 1957. *Freud and the Twentieth Century*. New York, Meridian Books.

Niebuhr, R. 1941. *The Nature and Destiny of Man*, 1. London, Nisbet.

Nietzsche, F. *WP. The Will to Power, Complete Works*, 14. Ed. O. Levy. Edinburgh and London, Foulis, 1909.

Nietzsche, F. *JW. The Joyful Wisdom, Complete Works*, 10. Ed. O. Levy. Edinburgh and London, Foulis, 1910.

Nietzsche, F. *GM. The Genealogy of Morals*. New York, Doubleday Anchor, 1956.

Nietzsche, F. *Z. Thus Spoke Zarathustra*. Harmondsworth, Penguin, 1961.

Nietzsche, F. *TF*. 'On Truth and Falsity in their Ultramoral Sense', *Complete Works*, 2. Ed. O. Levy. New York, Russell and Russell, 1964 (1909–11).

Nietzsche, F. *TI* and *A-X. Twilight of the Idols* and *The Antichrist*. Harmondsworth, Penguin, 1968.

Nietzsche, F. *BGE. Beyond Good and Evil.* Harmondsworth, Penguin, 1973.

Nietzsche, F. *EH. Ecce Homo.* Harmondsworth, Penguin, 1979.

Nietzsche, F. *D. Daybreak.* Cambridge, Cambridge University Press, 1982.

Nietzsche, F. *UM. Untimely Meditations.* Cambridge, Cambridge University Press, 1983.

Nietzsche, F. *HH. Human All Too Human.* Cambridge, Cambridge University Press, 1986.

Nietzsche, F. *BT. The Birth of Tragedy.* Harmondsworth, Penguin, 1993.

O'Flaherty, J. C., Sellner, T. F. and Helm, R. M. (eds.). 1985. *Studies in Nietzsche and the Judaeo-Christian Tradition.* Chapel Hill, University of North Carolina.

Pannenberg, W. 1971. *Basic Questions in Theology,* 2. London, SCM Press.

Pannenberg, W. 1976. *Theology and the Philosophy of Science.* London, Darton, Longman & Todd.

Pannenberg, W. 1985. *Anthropology in Theological Perspective.* Trans. M. J. O'Connell. Edinburgh, T & T Clark.

Pannenberg, W. 1992. *Systematic Theology,* 1. Edinburgh, T. & T. Clark.

Parekh, B. 1982. *Marx's Theory of Ideology.* London, Croom Helm.

Palsey, M. 1978. *Nietzsche: Imagery and Thought.* London, Methuen.

Perry, J. M. 1988. *Tillich's Response to Freud: A Christian Answer to the Freudian Critique of Religion.* Lanham, Md., University Press of America.

Peukert, H. 1984. *Science, Action and Fundamental Theology: Towards a Theology of Communicative Action.* Trans. J. Bohman, Massachusetts and London, MIT.

Pickering, W. S. F. 1984. *Durkheim's Sociology of Religion.* London, Routledge & Kegan Paul.

Plamenatz, J. 1975. *Karl Marx's Philosophy of Man.* Oxford, Clarendon Press.

Pletsch, C. 1991. *Young Nietzsche: Becoming a Genius.* New York, The Free Press.

Rahner, K. 1978. *Foundations of Christian Faith.* London, Darton, Longman & Todd, and New York, Seabury.

Rahner, K. *TI. Theological Investigations.* London, Darton, Longman & Todd. 1965–.

Ricoeur, P. 1970. *Freud and Philosophy.* New Haven, Yale University Press.

Rose, G. 1978. *The Melancholy Science.* London, Macmillan.

Rycroft, C. 1968. *A Critical Dictionary of Psychoanalysis.* London, Nelson.

Sassoon, S. 1984. *Collected Poems 1908–1956*. London, Faber & Faber.

Schacht. R. 1983. *Nietzsche*. London, Routledge & Kegan Paul.

Schaer, H. 1951. *Religion and the Cure of Souls in Jung's Psychology*. London, Routledge & Kegan Paul.

Scharfenberg, J. 1988. *Sigmund Freud – His Critique of Religion*. Philadelphia, Fortress Press.

Schleiermacher, F. D. E. 1928. *The Christian Faith*. Edinburgh, T & T Clark.

Seliger, M. M. 1977. *The Marxist Conception of Ideology*. Cambridge, Cambridge University Press.

Shelley, P. B. n.d. *Poems*. Edinburgh, Nelson.

Siebert, R. J. 1983. 'Adorno's Theory of Religion', *Telos*, 58 (1983–4), pp. 108–114.

Siebert, R. J. 1985. *The Critical Theory of Religion, The Frankfurt School*. Berlin etc., Mouton.

Skelton, R. (ed.). 1964. *Poetry of the Thirties*. Harmondsworth, Penguin.

Stern, J. P. 1979. *A Study of Nietzsche*. Cambridge, Cambridge University Press.

Storr, A. 1973. *Jung*. London, Fontana.

Surin, K. 1987, '*Contemptus Mundi* and the Disenchanted World: Bonhoeffer's "Discipline of the Secret" and Adorno's "Strategy of Hibernation" '. *Journal of the American Academy of Religion*, 53. pp. 383–410.

Tar, Z. 1977. *The Frankfurt School*. New York, Wiley.

Thomas, R. S. 1984. *Later Poems*. London, Macmillan.

Tillich, P. 1948. *The Protestant Era*. Chicago, University of Chicago Press.

Tillich, P. 1953. *Systematic Theology*, 3 vols in 1. Welwyn, Nisbet.

Tillich, P. 1964 (1959). *Theology and Culture*. New York, Oxford University Press.

Turner, D. 1983. *Marxism and Christianity*. Oxford, Basil Blackwell.

Van Herik, J. 1982. *Freud on Femininity and Faith*. Berkeley, Los Angeles and London, University of California Press.

Vico, G. 1961. *The New Science*. Trans. T. G. Bergin and M. H. Fisch, New York: Cornell University Press.

Vitz, P. C. 1993. *Sigmund Freud's Christian Unconscious* Grand Rapids, Eerdmans; Leominster, Grace-Wing.

von Franz, M.-L. 1980. *Projection and Re-Collection in Jungian Psychology*. La Salle, Open Court.

Wartofsky, M. 1977. *Feuerbach*. Cambridge, Cambridge University Press.

White, V. 1952. *God and the Unconscious*. London, Harvill.

Winnicot, D. W. 1985. *The Maturation Process and the Facilitating Environment*. London, Hogarth.

Index of Names